SECRET CODES

2005 VOL. 2

W9-BRC-267

GAME BOY® ADVANCE

Contents

ACE COMBAT ADVANCE

COMPLETE GAME WITH ALL PLANES AND LEVELS OPEN
Select Enter Code and enter QF9B9F59.

ALIENATORS: EVOLUTION CONTINUES

LEVEL 2
Enter MDKMZKCC as a password.

LEVEL 3
Enter BHSZSKTC as a password.

LEVEL 4
Enter ZKTSHKMC as a password.

LEVEL 5
Enter JLPFDKHB as a password.

LEVEL 6
Enter HMDBRKCB as a password.

LEVEL 7
Enter GLDKLKZB as a password.

LEVEL 8
Enter GLPKLKRB as a password.

LEVEL 9
Enter GLDJBKKF as a password.

LEVEL 10
Enter GLPJBKFF as a password.

LEVEL 11
Enter GLPKBKRF as a password.

LEVEL 12
Enter GLPKBKRF as a password.

LEVEL 13
Enter GLDJLKHD as a password.

UNLIMITED AMMO
Enter RBJPXCKC as a password.

ANIMAL SNAP: RESCUE THEM 2 BY 2

BLOCK BLASTER MINI-GAME
At the main menu, hold L and press Up, Down, Left, Right, Right, Left, Down, Up.

BIONICLE: TALES OF THE TOHUNGA

EVERYTHING BUT THE MINI-GAMES
Enter B9RBRN as a name.

GALI MINI-GAME
Enter 9MA268 as a name.

KOPAKA MINI-GAME
Enter V33673 as a name.

LEWA MINI-GAME
Enter 3LT154 as a name.

ONUA MINI-GAME
Enter 8MR472 as a name.

POHATU MINI-GAME
Enter 5MG834 as a name.

TAHU MINI-GAME
Enter 4CR487 as a name.

BUTT UGLY MARTIANS: B.K.M. BATTLES

UNLIMITED LIVES
Enter KMIORMAO as a password.

MAX DEFENSE, FIREPOWER AND RESTORATION PICKUPS
Enter ALWMAA15 as a password.

2 DEFENSE UPGRADES
Enter JT2DU 4MP as a password.

2 EXTRA LIVES
Enter 2ELFM PLS as a password.

2 WEAPON UPGRADES
Enter GMACO EWU as a password.

4 DEFENSE UPGRADES
Enter DUATO U4M as a password.

4 EXTRA LIVES
Enter IAGAW 4EL as a password.

4 WEAPON UPGRADES
Enter IAGAW 4WU as a password.

START AT MECHTROPOLIS
Select Resume Game and enter IWTSOWN2.

START AT AQUATICA
Select Resume Game and enter TMTWN3PD.

START AT ARBOREA
Select Resume Game and enter IIALTSMO4.

START AT SILICON CITY
Select Resume Game and enter IOTJOWN5.

START AT MAGMA
Select Resume Game and enter FILGSOW6.

START AT KOO FOO SHIP
Select Resume Game and enter IWTSOWN7.

CAR BATTLER JOE

JIM JOE ZERO CAR
In Battle League, enter TODOROKI as a password.

CARTOON NETWORK SPEEDWAY

UNLOCK EVERYTHING
Enter 96981951 as a password.

ALL FIVE CHAMPIONSHIPS COMPLETE
Enter 34711154 as a password.

START AT FARM FROLICS
Enter 12761357 as a password.

START AT DOWN ON THE FARM
Enter 25731079 as a password.

START AT MURIEL
Enter 25731079 as a password.

START AT EDOPOLIS
Enter 38611791 as a password.

START AT JOHNNY 2X4
Enter 52681314 as a password.

START AT SCARY SPEEDWAY
Enter 68851752 as a password.

START AT DESERT DRIVE
Enter 81821475 as a password.

START AT LITTLE SUZY
Enter 81821475 as a password.

START AT HOT ROD JOHNNY
Enter 84891097 as a password.

START AT SWANKY
Enter 98761719 as a password.

START AT ALPINE ANTICS
Enter 98761719 as a password.

ACME AXEL AWARD TROPHY
Enter 50000050 as a password.

CARTOON SPEEDWAY TROPHY
Enter 10000010 as a password.

FENDER BENDER FRENZY TROPHY
Enter 32000010 as a password.

CASTLEVANIA: ARIA OF SORROW

Enter the following codes as a name, then start a new game:

USE NO SOULS
Enter NOSOUL.

USE NO ITEMS
Enter NOUSE.

PLAY AS JULIUS BELMONT
After defeating the game with a good ending, enter JULIUS.

CLASSIC NES SERIES: BOMBERMAN

LEVEL PASSWORDS

LEVEL	PASSWORD
01	NMIHPPBPCAFHABDPCPCH
02	HIJDIJFJDLHFLOPDJDJN
03	BAJDINANMJGGCPOOLOLG
04	DJOLBGLGKGJAHIEMNMNN
05	NMKGDDONMHLCGKKGKGKJ
06	ABGKKBPHILHFLOPCPCPC
07	FEBABGLEFLHFLOPCPCPA
08	HIFEMIIABJGGCPOBABAN
09	NMEFPHCMNJGGCPOBABAF
10	JDGKKBPHILHFLOPGKGKL
11	HIPCOHCMNLHFLOPEFEFG
12	ABJDIFJKGGJAHIEPCPCN
13	JDBABANOLJGGCPODJDJF
14	ABNMKNAIHFAJNMMKGKGF
15	ABIHPGLEFCNNJDBEFEFN
16	ABABEMKJDAFHABDCPPCN
17	JDDJOIIOLCNNJDBABOLH
18	JDNMKLGHILHFLOPGKEFH
19	DJABEKMPCFAJNMMOLFEL
20	FEGKKJFNMAFHABDABOLN
21	NMKGDDOIHJGGCPONMIHN
22	NMCPIIIOLFAJNMMGKEFF
23	NMPCOIIOLCNNJDBBAHIJ
24	NMGKKEEHILHFLOPPCGKL
25	HIKGDODCPGJAHIEPCGKJ
26	ABHIMGLBANCLFEINMIHH
27	MNGKKDOOLGJAHIEKGCPC
28	OLDJOIIKGLHFLOPEFLOL
29	IHJDIKMEFNCLFEINMIHF
30	IHDJOIIKGLHFLOPMNJDA
31	DJJDIDOOLFAJNMMEFLOC

LEVEL	PASSWORD
32	IHIHPBPCPNCBOLIHIJDH
33	OLFEMANMNFADDJMABFEF
34	MNDJOODJDHLPPCKBAMNA
35	DJABEMKMNNCMIHIMNDJC
36	BADJOIIIHAFDDJDIHOLA
37	DJFEMPBPCGJKEFEEFBAC
38	DJKGDIIIHJGBOLOABFEH
39	DJCPIODFECNOBABABFEN
40	IHEFPPPBGKFAIMNMOLKGJ
41	IHLOEHCMNNCMIHIHOLJ
42	DJEFPHCMNJGBOLOABFEH
43	MNGKKIIOLGJKEFEKGPCJ
44	BAPCOMKDJJGBOLODJIHJ
45	OLNMKDOIHFAIMNMGKLOF
46	OLIHPMKNMFAIMNMABFEH
47	OLABEMKNMCNOBABPCEFL
48	OLOLBFJGKGJKEFEFEPCL
49	OLFEMFJGKLHPPCPLOMNL
50	NMABEKMKGNCLFEIIHFEL

CLASSIC NES SERIES: THE LEGEND OF ZELDA

SECOND QUEST
Enter ZELDA as a name.

CLASSIC NES SERIES: METROID

EVERYTHING
Enter JUSTIN BAILEY as a password.

INVINCIBILITY AND UNLIMITED MISSILES
Enter NARPAS SWORD0 000000 000000 as a password.

CRASH BANDICOOT PURPLE: RIPTO'S RAMPAGE

100 WUMPA
At the Mode menu, press L + R, then enter CR4SH.

200 WUMPA
At the Mode menu, press L + R, then enter G3CK0.

500 WUMPA
At the Mode menu, press L + R, then enter C0FF33.

ORANGE GAME
At the Mode menu, press L + R, then enter L4MPP0ST.

GREEN PANTS
At the Mode menu, press L + R, then enter K1LL4Z.

GRENADES
At the Mode menu, press L + R, then enter STR4WB3RRY. Use the R Button to toss grenades.

SPYRO PARTY MINI-GAME
Turn on your Game Boy Advance and hold L + R.

CREDITS
At the Mode menu, press L + R, then enter CR3D1TS.

CRASH NITRO KART

CRASH PARTY USA MINI-GAME
Hold L + R and turn on the game.

 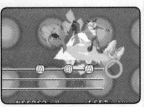

CRUIS'N VELOCITY

UNLOCK EVERYTHING
Enter RLCRHVGD as a password.

PASSWORDS
Enter the following as a password:

LEVEL	PASSWORD
Amateur Cup	HLDDRTSN
Pro Cup	HLDDSNST
Velocity Cup	HLDDNRLN
Championship	HLDDHVGD

DISNEY'S HOME ON THE RANGE

LEVEL 1
Enter DVHB as a password.

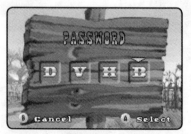

LEVEL 2
Enter VCFK as a password.

LEVEL 3
Enter BQMF as a password.

LEVEL 4
Enter HFKM as a password.

LEVEL 5
Enter DMCV as a password.

LEVEL 6
Enter BBKD as a password.

LEVEL 7
Enter KNLC as a password.

LEVEL 8
Enter BDJR as a password.

LEVEL 9
Enter BDRN as a password.

LEVEL 10
Enter PSBH as a password.

LEVEL 11
Enter QRNN as a password.

LEVEL 12
Enter MMKN as a password.

LEVEL 13
Enter PSFH as a password.

LEVEL 14
Enter DBVJ as a password.

DONKEY KONG COUNTRY

50 LIVES
At the game select, highlight Erase. Then hold Select and press B, A, R, R, A, L.

DONKEY KONG COUNTRY 2: DIDDY KONG'S QUEST

ALL LEVELS
Select Cheats from the Options and enter freedom.

START WITH 15 LIVES
Select Cheats from the Options and enter helpme.

START WITH 55 LIVES
Select Cheats from the Options and enter weakling.

START WITH 10 BANANA COINS
Select Cheats from the Options and enter richman.

START WITH 50 BANANA COINS
Select Cheats from the Options and enter wellrich.

NO DK OR HALF WAY BARRELS
Select Cheats from the Options and enter rockard.

MUSIC PLAYER
Select Cheats from the Options and enter onetime.

CREDITS
Select Cheats from the Options and enter kredits.

DORA THE EXPLORER: SUPER SPIES

RAINFOREST 2 PASSWORD
Select Continue and enter Arrow up, Plus sign, Triangle, Star, Plus sign, Triangle, Frown.

FINAL FANTASY I & II: DAWN OF SOULS

FF I TILE GAME
During a game of Final Fantasy I and after you get the ship, hold A and press B about 55 times.

FF II CONCENTRATION GAME
Once you obtain the Snowcraft, hold B and press A about 20 times.

GRADIUS GALAXIES

SLOWER
Pause the game and press Left, Right, Up, Down, Left, Left, Right, Start.

SELF-DESTRUCT
Pause the game and press Up, Up, Down, Down, Left, Right, Left, Right, B, A, Start.

GT ADVANCE 3: PRO CONCEPT RACING

ALL CARS
At the Title screen, hold L + B and press Left.

ALL TRACKS
At the Title screen, hold L + B and press Right.

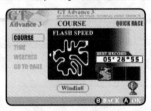

ALL TUNE UPS
At the Title screen, hold L + B and press Up.

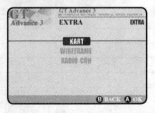

EXTRA MODES
At the Title screen, hold L + B and press Down.

HOT WHEELS VELOCITY X

PASSWORDS

LEVEL	PASSWORD	LEVEL	PASSWORD
02	143-24-813	21	766-46-341
03	141-38-985	22	187-98-394
04	249-48-723	23	188-12-234
05	294-16-277	24	786-84-747
06	457-51-438	25	466-59-979
07	112-86-545	26	477-58-369
08	447-65-112	27	447-62-191
09	368-54-466	28	614-81-432
10	718-59-438	29	641-18-239
11	363-95-545	30	399-68-584
12	373-65-848	31	662-84-635
13	171-49-211	32	476-63-843
14	373-59-216	33	616-67-341
15	373-62-927	34	384-97-475
16	718-42-276	35	363-13-298
17	358-59-355	36	521-71-135
18	478-68-254	37	543-17-658
19	573-77-683	38	782-57-387
20	188-58-352		

THE INCREDIBLE HULK

STAGE SKIP
Pause the game and press Down, Right, Down, Right, Left, Left, Left, Up.

THE INCREDIBLES

PASSWORDS

LEVEL	PASSWORD	LEVEL	PASSWORD
1-1-1	MSW5	2-5-2	6?SR
1-1-2	BK8V	2-5-3	SNJ5
1-2-1	69NN	3-1-1	MNW9
1-3-1	GFVY	3-2-1	BF8Z
1-3-2	V34K	3-2-2	65NS
2-1-1	94HR	3-2-3	YVKK
2-1-2	ZWLG	3-2-4	KGTY
2-1-3	SP??	3-3-1	SDR6
2-2-1	KDY3	3-4-1	Z3ZB
2-3-1	Y27F	3-5-1	9?5M
2-3-2	6!2N	3-5-2	FC73
2-3-3	BHBV	3-5-3	NL2?
2-4-1	MQR5	3-6-1	VXBG
2-4-2	3YTK	3-6-2	YWKJ
2-4-3	?6DS	3-6-3	GJQZ

LEVEL	PASSWORD	LEVEL	PASSWORD
3-7-1	KHP2	4-3-1	YXFC
3-7-2	313K	4-4-1	GHV1
4-1-1	?!JT	4-5-1	VW4C
4-2-1	ML17	4-6-1	YX!F

JAZZ JACKRABBIT

500 CREDITS
Pause the game and press Right, Left, Right, Left, L, R, Up, Up, R, R, L, L.

1000 CREDITS
Pause the game and press Up, Down, Up, Down, Left, Right, L, R, L, R, R, L.

5000 CREDITS
Pause the game and press Up, Right, Down, Left, L, L, Right, Left, R, R, L, L.

JUSTICE LEAGUE: INJUSTICE FOR ALL

CAN'T BE HIT
Pause the game, press Select and Unpause.

KONAMI COLLECTOR'S SERIES: ARCADE ADVANCED

FROGGER: ADVANCED
At the Frogger title screen, press Up (x2), Down (x2), Left, Right, Left, Right, B, A, Start.

SCRAMBLE: ADVANCED
At the Scramble title screen, press Up (x2), Down (x2), Left, Right, Left, Right, B, A, Start.

TIME PILOT: RAPID FIRE AND NEW STAGE
At the Time Pilot title screen, press Up (x2), Down (x2), Left, Right, Left, Right, B, A, Start.

GYRUSS: ADVANCED
At the Gyruss title screen, press Up (x2), Down (x2), Left, Right, Left, Right, B, A, Start.

YIE-AR KUNG FU: ALL FIGHTERS IN MULTIPLAYER
At the Yie Ar Kung Fu title screen, press Up (x2), Down (x2), Left, Right, Left, Right, B, A, Start.

RUSH N' ATTACK: 2 EXTRA LIVES AND 2 NEW STAGES
At the Rush N' Attack title screen, press Up (x2), Down (x2), Left, Right, Left, Right, B, A, Start.

LEGO KNIGHT'S KINGDOM

STORY 100% COMPLETE
Enter YZZVZYZ as a password.

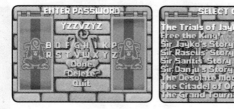

LEGO STAR WARS

SHEEP MODE
Pause the game and press L, R, L, Down, Up, R, R, Right, Left, Down, Right, Right, Select

YODA SAYS
Pause the game and press Down, L, R, Select.

WATCH CUTSCENES
Pause the game and press Down, Up, R, L, R, R, R, Down, Down, Up, Down, Down, Select.

REPAIR BOT

Pause the game and press Down, Down, Down, Down, L, Right, Down, Right, L.

TEMPORARY SPEED BOOST

Pause the game and press Right, Right, Down, Up, Right, L.

PLAY AS BATTLE DROID

On the start screen, Start, Start, Left, Down, Down, Down, Down, Right.

PLAY AS A DROIDEKA

Pause the game and press Start, Start, Down, Right, Left, Down, Right, Left.

PLAY AS A REPAIR DROID

Pause the game and press Start, Start, Up, Up, Up, Down, Down, Down.

PLAY AS BLUE GUNGAN
Pause the game and press Start, Start, Down, Left, Right, Down, Left, Right.

PLAY AS C-3PO
Pause the game and press press Start, Start, Left, Down, Right, Up, Right, Right.

PLAY AS DROID ON HOVERSLED
Pause the game and press Start, Start, Down, Up, Down, Up, Down, Up.

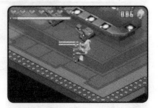

PLAY AS GENERAL GRIEVOUS
Pause the game and press Start, Start, Down, Down, Down, Down, Down, Down.

PLAY AS WINGED GUY
Pause the game and press Start, Start, Right, Down, Right, Down, Left, Up.

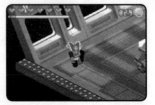

PLAY AS R2-D2
Pause the game and press Start, Start, Up, Up, Up, Up, Up, Up.

PLAY AS R4-P17
Pause the game and press Start, Start, Up, Down, Up, Down, Up, Down.

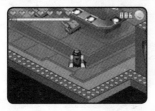

POWERFUL BLASTERS
Pause the game and press Down, Down, Left, Right, Down, L.

A FEW LEGO PIECES
Pause the game and press L, L, L, Right, Left, R, R, R.

BLACK SABER
Pause the game and press L, L, R, Start.

BLUE SABER

Pause the game and press R, R, R, Start.

GREEN SABER

Pause the game and press R, L, R, Start.

PURPLE SABER

Pause the game and press L, R, L, Start.

RED SABER

Pause the game and press L, R, R, Start.

YELLOW SABER

Pause the game and press R, R, L, Start.

MEGA MAN BATTLE NETWORK 3

ERROR CODES

If you attempt to use a Program of a color your current Style does not support, you will get an Error and be unable to boot up MegaMan until the problem is fixed.

You can bypass these Error once you have purchased the ModTools at Beach Street. When the Error number appears, press Select and input the Code to counter. But this only works if you have the proper Code for the specific Error. Error codes can be obtained by talking to the right people or reading BBSes, or looking at this list below.

ERROR	CODE	ERROR	CODE
A3	LO13ZXME	F3	ITA2CRWQ
B2	ALSK3W2R	G2C	TIS1LAEJ
B3	Y2UOMNCB	G2G	CVVDS2WR
B5	BM2KWIRA	H2	UTIW2SMF
C2	UTIXM1LA	S2C	TU1AW2LL
D2G	OI1UWMAN	S2G	AX1RTDS3
E1	P2I3MSJL	S2S	F2AAFETG

MOD CODES

The ModTools can be used for more than just fixing program errors. With a properly-programmed MegaMan, hit Select when the "OK!" appears, then enter in a code from the list below for an added Program effect without taking up valuable real estate!

CODE	EFFECT
JIEU1AWT	HP+100
ZBKDEU1W	Block
UIEU2NGO	DashRun
PEOTIR2G	FlotShoe
SJH1UEKA	Humor
JDKGJ1U2	MegFldr1

COMPRESSION CODES

Speaking of valuable real estate, the ModTools can be used in ways even Dad Hikari was unaware of. Highlight a Program in the list, then press and hold Select. Enter the right combination of buttons, and the Program will be compressed slightly, allowing you room for more Programs in the grid!

PROGRAM	COMPRESS CODE
BlckMind	Right, Left, Right, Down, R, Down
BrakChrg	B, A, Left, L, Up, B
BugStop	B, Down, Up, B, Down, B
Collect	B, Down, Right, R, Right, Right
DashRun	R, L, B, Down, Down, Down
Humor	Up, R, A, Left, Right, Right
MegFdlr2	A, R, Down, Down, Right, Left
OilBody	Up, Right, A, A, R, Up
SetMetl	B, R, Right, Right, L, L
SprArmor	Up, Right, Up, R, Up, Down

MEGA MAN BATTLE NETWORK 4

BATTLE CHIP CHALLENGE CODES

If you've been exploring everything, you should have acquired six NaviCodes. This chart lists them all, plus a special seventh code that gives you a shot at acquiring Chip #229, the HubStyle NaviChip!

NAME	NAVICODE
LAN	NG75-H5RF-R0MN-440N-2QX♣-X341
MAYL	8NT8-JZFL-3Q9D-7RPX-T♦CH-JX51
DEX	FD♠3-3JW1-PS♠V-♦01♦-♥6R♣-1J32
CHAU	93♣5-WXNH-9MWT-♠VX8-DY7M-88H0
KAI	M♠SP-3♥♦C-6KGQ-♥9FM-X0N♥-M♦P1
MARY	CX4♠-1GA9-5JKL-S♣GD-3L5B-90Z1
LAN	5♠4H-B81R-♠KKZ-P15X-ZS5B-♣XK0

MLB SLUGFEST 20-04

CHEATS

Enter the following codes at the Matchup screen using the B, A, and R buttons. For example, for All Fielders Run (132 Up), press B once, A three times, and R twice, then press Up.

EFFECT	CODE
1920 Mode	242 Up
All Fielders Run	132 Up
Backwards Fielders	444 Right
Fireworks	141 Right
Ghost Fielders	313 Down
Nuke Ball	343 Up
Skull Ball	323 Left

MONSTER FORCE

RESTART LEVEL
Pause the game, hold L + R and press A.

FINISH LEVEL
During a game, hold L + R + A and press Up.

PLAY AS MINA OR DREW

At the Character Select, hold L + R + B and press Right.

RIVER CITY RANSOM EX

Select the status menu and change your name to the following:

MAX STATS
DAMAX

$999999.99
PLAYA

CUSTOM CHAR
XTRA0

CUSTOM SELF
XTRA1

CUSTOM MOVE
XTRA2

CLEAR SAVE
ERAZE

TECHNIQUES 1
FUZZY. This group includes Mach Punch, Dragon Kick, Acro Circus, Grand Slam, Javelin Man, Slick Trick, Nitro Port, Twin Kick, Deadly Shot, Top Spin, Helicopter, Torpedo.

TECHNIQUES 2
WUZZY. This group includes Slap Happy, Pulper, Headbutt, Kickstand, Big Bang, Wheel Throw, Glide Chop, Head Bomb, Chain Chump, Jet Kick, Shuriken, Flip Throw

TECHNIQUES 3

WAZZA. This group includes Boomerang, Charge It, Bat Fang, Flying Kick, Speed Drop, Bomb Blow, Killer Kick, Bike Kick, Slam Punk, Dragon Knee, God Fist, Hyperguard.

TECHNIQUES 4

BEAR*. This group includes PhoenixWing, Inlines, Springlines, Rocketeers, Air Merc's Narcishoes, Magic Pants, Pandora Box, Skaterz, Custom Fit.

ROAD RASH: JAILBREAK

ALL CHARACTERS AT LEVEL 4 AND ALL RACES

Press Select at the Player select and enter ALAKAZAMM.

ALL RACES

Press Select at the Player select and enter KEEPOUT.

ALL RACES IN COP PATROL

Press Select at the Player select and enter FELONY.

SURVIVAL

Press Select at the Player select and enter MENACE.

ACE LEVEL 2

Press Select at the Player select and enter SWING.

ACE LEVEL 3

Press Select at the Player select and enter FLUSH.

ACE LEVEL 4

Press Select at the Player select and enter BRUISE.

FAT HOAGIE

Press Select at the Player select and enter EDGY.

FAT HOAGIE LEVEL 2

Press Select at the Player select and enter SLAP.

FAT HOAGIE LEVEL 3

Press Select at the Player select and enter FURIOUS.

FAT HOAGIE LEVEL 4

Press Select at the Player select and enter HEADACHE.

HURL LEVEL 1

Press Select at the Player select and enter HOWDY.

HURL LEVEL 2

Press Select at the Player select and enter PULSE.

HURL LEVEL 3

Press Select at the Player select and enter STRIDER.

HURL LEVEL 4
Press Select at the Player select and enter BEATNIK.

LULU LEVEL 2
Press Select at the Player select and enter BLOW.

LULU LEVEL 3
Press Select at the Player select and enter SCOURGE.

LULU LEVEL 4
Press Select at the Player select and enter QUICKEN.

TINY LEVEL 2
Press Select at the Player select and enter AXLE.

TINY LEVEL 3
Press Select at the Player select and enter WHEEL.

TINY LEVEL 4
Press Select at the Player select and enter PROPER.

ROAD TRIP: SHIFTING GEARS

DRAGON PARTS
Complete the Angel Cup. Select Change Name from the Options and enter DRAGON.

RUGRATS: I GOTTA GO PARTY

GO TO LEVEL 2
Enter CBKBBB as a password.

GO TO LEVEL 3
Enter RBHBNB as a password.

GO TO LEVEL 4
Enter SNFBBC as a password.

GO TO LEVEL 5
Enter TNHHBG as a password.

GO TO LEVEL 6
Enter VNFTNG as a password.

GO TO LEVEL 7
Enter XNHTFC as a password.

GO TO LEVEL 8
Enter ZNFTRJ as a password.

SECRET AGENT BARBIE: ROYAL JEWELS MISSION

ALL SECRETS
Enter TTTTTS as a password.

ENGLAND – THE ROYAL TOWER
Enter BBBBCG as a password.

ENGLAND – STREET CHASE
Enter DBBFCM as a password.

CHINA – CITY STREETS
Enter FBBFFQ as a password.

CHINA – SECRET HIDEOUT
Enter GBBPFH as a password.

CHINA – GOLDEN CITY
Enter HBBPKN as a password.

CHINA – THE PALACE
Enter JCBPKQ as a password.

ITALY – OPERA HOUSE
Enter KCBTKC as a password.

ITALY - CANAL CHASE
Enter LCGTKJ as a password.

ITALY – FASHION DISTRICT
Enter MCHTKL as a password.

ITALY – SCUBA SEARCH
Enter NCHTTC as a password.

MEXICO - SUNNY CITY
Enter PCRTTN as a password.

SHAMAN KING:
LEGACY OF THE SPIRITS - SOARING HAWK

SPIRIT OF FIRE
At the title screen, press Right, Right, L, Left + R, Down, R, Right, B.

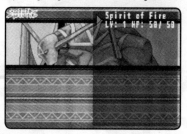

SHAMAN KING:
LEGACY OF THE SPIRITS - SPRINTING WOLF

SPIRIT OF FIRE
At the title screen, press Right, Right, L, Left + R, Down, R, Right, B.

SHINING SOUL

2 EXTRA HERBS
Enter your name as Shining.

2 VALUING SCROLLS
Enter your name as Force.

HEALING DROP
Enter your name as Soul.

MONKEY DOLL
Enter your name as AiAi.

PAINTER'S SOUL
Enter your name as Salamander.

JUDO UNIFORM FOR DRAGONUTE
Select the Dragonute and enter your name as Segata.

LEAF BRIEFS FOR ARCHER
Select the Archer and enter your name as NomuNomu.

SHINING SOUL II

DREAM HAT
Enter Nindri as your name.

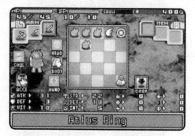

GENOME RING
Enter Genomes as your name.

ATLUS RING
Enter Vjum as your name.

POWER GLOVES
Enter VJxSS as your name.

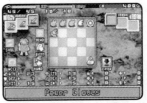

STR +5
Enter Ninky as your name.

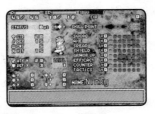

DEX +5
Enter Yoshi as your name.

VIT +5
Enter Taicho as your name.

INT +5, RTH +30
Enter Dengeki as your name.

RDK +30
Enter Montaka as your name.

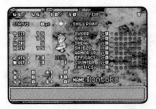

RFR +30
Enter Iyoku as your name.

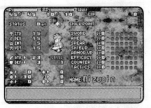

RIC +30
Enter Mizupin as your name.

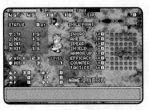

RPO +30
Enter Hachi as your name.

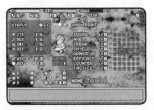

SPIDER-MAN 2

INVINCIBILITY
At the title screen, press Up, Down, Right, A.

LEVEL SELECT
After completing the game, start a new game with the name FLUWDEAR.

SPYRO ORANGE: THE CORTEX CONSPIRACY

100 GEMS
At the Mode menu, press L + R, then enter V1S10NS.

ORANGE GAME
At the Mode menu, press L + R, then enter SP4RX.

PURPLE GAME
At the Mode menu, press L + R, then enter PORT4L.

ORANGE SPYRO
At the Mode menu, press L + R, then enter SPYRO.

SHEEP MODE
At the Mode menu, press L + R, then enter SH33P.

SHEEP FLAME MODE
At the Mode menu, press L + R, then enter B41SOKV.

CRASH PARTY USA MINI-GAME
Start up your Game Boy Advance and hold L + R.

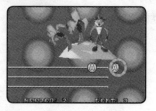

STREET FIGHTER ALPHA 3

ALL FIGHTERS
At the title screen, press Left, Right, Down, Right, L, L, A, L, L, B, R, A, Up.

ALL MODES
At the title screen, press A, Up, A, L, R, Right, L, Right, A, Down, Right.
Now press L, Right, A, R, Up, L, Right, B, A, Up, Right, Down, Right.

PLAY AS SUPER BISON
At the character select, hold Start and select Bison.

PLAY AS SHIN AKUMA
At the character select, hold Start and select Akuma.

ALTERNATE COSTUMES
At the character select, press L or R.

FINAL BATTLE
At the speed select, hold A + B.

SUPER MONKEY BALL JR.

ENABLE ALL
At the title screen, press Down, Down, Up, Up, Left, Right, Left, Right, B, A.

BLOCKY MODE
At the title screen, press Left, Left, Right, Right, Down, Down, A.

NICE TRY
At the title screen, press Up, Up, Down, Down, Left, Right, Left, Right, B, A.

SUPER PUZZLE FIGHTER 2 TURBO

AKUMA PLAYER 1
Highlight Morrigan, hold Select, press Down (3x), Left (3x), A.

AKUMA PLAYER 2
Highlight Felicia, hold Select, press Down (3x), Right (3x), A.

ANITA PLAYER 1
Highlight Morrigan, hold Select, move to Donovan and press A.

ANITA PLAYER 2
Highlight Felicia, hold Select, move to Donovan and press A.

DAN PLAYER 1
Highlight Morrigan, hold Select, press Left (3x), Down (3x), A.

DAN PLAYER 2
Highlight Felicia, hold Select, press Right (3x), Down (3x), A

DEVILOT
Highlight Morrigan, hold Select, press Left (3x), Down (3x), A as the timer hits 10.

HSIEN-KO'S PAPER TALISMAN PLAYER 1
Highlight Morrigan, hold Select, move to Hsien-Ko and press A.

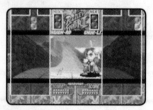

HSIEN-KO'S PAPER TALISMAN PLAYER 2
Highlight Felicia, hold Select, move to Hsien-Ko and press A.

TONY HAWK'S UNDERGROUND

SKIP TUTORIAL
At the Main Menu, hold R and press Left, Down, Start, Start, Right, Up, Up, L, Down.

TONY HAWK'S UNDERGROUND 2

TENNIS SHOOTER MINIGAME
Once you unlock Bam's character on the map, talk to him. Knock down the rollerbladers, then go back. He'll give you the Tennis Shooter minigame. Once you've completed three levels, save your game to access Tennis Shooter at any time from the main menu.

TRON 2.0: KILLER APP

ALL MINIGAMES
At the title screen, press Left, Left, Left, Left, Up, Right, Down, Down, Select.

URBAN YETI

UNLOCK EVERYTHING
Enter TONYGOLD as a password

START AT LEVEL 1
Enter BUZZWORD as a password.

START AT LEVEL 2
Enter FOREWORD as a password.

START AT LEVEL 3
Enter COOKBOOK as a password.

START AT LEVEL 4
Enter FEEDBAGS as a password.

START AT LEVEL 5
Enter HAMSTEAK as a password.

START AT LEVEL 6
Enter DAYBREAK as a password.

START AT LEVEL 7
Enter SUNLIGHT as a password.

START AT LEVEL 8
Enter NITETIME as a password.

START AT LEVEL 9
Enter EASTSIDE as a password.

START AT LEVEL 10
Enter BEATDOWN as a password.

START AT LEVEL 11
Enter VENGEFUL as a password.

START AT LEVEL 12
Enter FRISBEES as a password.

START AT LEVEL 13
Enter ICESKATE as a password.

START AT LEVEL 14
Enter PINGPONG as a password.

START AT LEVEL 15
Enter DOWNTOWN as a password.

START AT LEVEL 16
Enter CITYMAPS as a password.

START AT LEVEL 17
Enter DUMPSTER as a password.

START AT LEVEL 18
Enter WATERWAY as a password.

START AT LEVEL 19
Enter TIRETUBE as a password.

START AT LEVEL 20
Enter YETIRAFT as a password.

START AT LEVEL 21
Enter SUBURBIA as a password.

START AT LEVEL 22
Enter HOUSETOP as a password.

START AT LEVEL 23
Enter CITIZENS as a password.

START AT LEVEL 24
Enter CHICKENS as a password.

START AT LEVEL 25
Enter SONGBIRD as a password.

START AT LEVEL 26
Enter PROVIDER as a password.

STRANGE COLORS AND SOUND
Enter BSWSBSWS as a password

THE URBZ: SIMS IN THE CITY

CLUB XIZZLE
Once you gain access to Club Xizzle, enter with the password "bucket."

WORLD CHAMPIONSHIP POKER

10 MILLION DOLLARS
Enter the following as a password: 7 Hearts, King Spades, 2 Hearts, Queen Clubs, 9 Hearts, Jack Hearts.

YU-GI-OH! 7 TRIALS TO GLORY: WORLD CHAMPIONSHIP TOURNAMENT 2005

PURPLE TITLE SCREEN
Completing the game changes the title screen from blue to purple. To switch it back, press Up, Up, Down, Down, Left, Right, Left, Right, B, A at the title screen.

CREDITS
Defeat the game. Then, press Up, Up, Down, Down, Left, Right, Left, Right, B, A.

CARD PASSWORDS
At the password machine, press R and enter the following.

CARD	PASSWORD	CARD	PASSWORD
30,000-Year White Turtle	11714098	Ancient Brain	42431843
7 Colored Fish	23771716	Ancient Elf	93221206
7 Completed	86198326	Ancient Lizard Warrior	43230671
A Hero Emerges	21597117	Anti Raigeki	42364257
Acid Trap Hole	41356845	Aqua Chorus	95132338
Air Eater	08353769	Aqua Dragon	86164529
Airknight Parshath	18036057	Archfiend Soldier	49881766
Alligator's Sword	64428736	Arma Knight	36151751
Alligator's Sword Dragon	03366982	Armaill	53153481
Alpha The Magnet Warrior	99785935	Armed Ninja	09076207
Amazon Archer	91869203	Armored Lizard	15480588
Amazon of the Seas	17968114	Armored Rat	16246527
Amphibian Beast	67371383	Armored Starfish	17535588
Amphibious Bugroth	40173854	Armored Zombie	20277860
Amphibious Bugroth MK-3	64342551	Axe of Despair	40619825

CARD	PASSWORD
Axe Raider	48305365
Baby Dragon	88819587
Backup Soildier	36280194
Banisher of the Light	61528025
Baron of the Fiend Sword	86325596
Barrel Dragon	81480460
Barrel Lily	67841515
Barrel Rock	10476868
Beaver Warrior	32452818
Beta The Magnet Warrior	39256679
Bite Shoes	50122883
Black Luster Soldier - Envoy of the Beginning	72989439
Black Luster Soldier - EotB	72989439
Black Pendant	65169794
Bladefly	28470714
Blast Sphere	26302522
Blazing Inpachi	05464695
Blue Eyes Toon Dragon	53183600
Blue Eyes White Dragon	89631139
Boneheimer	98456117
Book of Moon	14087893
Book of SecretArts	91595718
Bottom Dweller	81386177
Buster Blader	78193831
Call of the Haunted	97077563
Card Destruction	72892473
Catapult Turtle	95727991
Ceasefire	36468556
Celtic Guardian	91152256
Ceremonial Bell	20228463
Chain Destruction	01248895
Change of Heart	04031928
Chaos Emperor Dragon - EotE	82301904
Cliff The Trap Remover	06967870
Confiscation	17375316
Contract with the Dark Master	96420087
Contract With The Dark Master	96420087
Crass Clown	93889755
Crimson Ninja	14618326
Curse of Dragon	28279543
Curse of the Masked Beast	94377247
Cyber Falcon	30655537
Cyber Harpie	80316585

CARD	PASSWORD
Cyber Jar	34124316
Cyber Shield	63224564
Cyber Soldier of Darkworld	75559356
Cyber-Stein	69015963
Cyber-Tech Alligator	48766543
D.D Assaliant	70074904
D.D. Warrior Lady	07572887
Dark Artist	72520073
Dark Blade	11321183
Dark Hole	53129443
Dark Illusion Ritual	41426869
Dark Magician Girl	38033121
Dark Magician of Chaos	40737112
Dark Master Zorc	97642679
Dark Room of Nightmare	85562745
Dark Scorpion-Chick The Yellow	61587183
Dark Scorpion-Gorg The Strong	48768179
Dark Snake Syndrome	47233801
Dark-Eyes Illusionist	38247752
Darkfire Soldier #1	05388481
Darkfire Soldier #2	78861134
Darkmaster - Zorc	97642679
De-Spell	19159413
Deepsea Warrior	24128274
Des Koala	69579761
Destiny Board	94212438
Destroyer Golem	73481154
Dissolverock	40826495
Disturbance Strategy	77561728
Don Zaloog	76922029
Dragon Manipulator	63018132
Dragonic Attack	32437102
Dream Clown	13215230
Dunames Dark Witch	12493482
Eatgaboon	42578427
Exile of the Wicked	26725158
Exiled Force	74131780
Exodia the Forbidden One	33396948
Fiber Jar	78706415
Fiend Reflection #2	02863439
Final Countdown	95308449
Final Destiny	18591904
Fire Princess	64752646
Firegrass	53293545

CARD	PASSWORD
Flame Champion	42599677
Flame Swordsman	45231177
Flash Assailant	96890582
Flower Wolf	95952802
Flying Kamakiri #1	84834865
Flying Kamakiri #2	03134241
Freed The Brave Wanderer	16556849
Freed The Matchless General	49681811
Fushi No Tori	38538445
Gagagigo	49003308
Gaia the Fierce Knight	06368038
Gamma The Magnet Warrior	11549357
Garnecia Elefantis	49888191
Gearfried The Iron Knight	00423705
Gemini Elf	69140098
Giant Flea	41762634
Giant Orc (Oak)	73698349
Giant Rat	97017120
Giant Soldier of Stone	13039848
Gift of the Mystical Elf	98299011
Goblin Attack Force	78658564
Goblin Fan	04149689
Graceful Charity	79571449
Graceful Dice	74137509
Graverobber's Retribution	33737664
Gravity Bind	85742772
Great Long Nose	02356994
Great White	13429800
Guardian Sphinx	40659562
Harpie Lady	76812113
Harpie's Feather Duster	18144506
Hayabusa Knight	21015833
Headless Knight	05434080
Heavy Storm	19613556
Hino-Kagu-Tsuchi	75745607
Humanoid Worm Drake	05600127
Hyosube	02118022
Hyozanryu	62397231
Illusion Wall	13945283
Inaba White Rabbit	77084837
Iron Blacksmith Kotetsu	73431236
Jar of Greed	83968380
Jellyfish	14851496
Jigen Bakudan	90020065
Jinzo	77585513
Jowgen the Spiritualist	41855169

CARD	PASSWORD
Karate Man	23289281
Kojikocy	01184620
Kuriboh	40640057
Kycoo the Ghost Destroyer	88240808
La Jinn	97590747
Lady of Faith	17358176
Lady Panther	38480590
Last Day of Witch	90330453
Lava Battleguard	20394040
Left Arm of the Forbidden One	07902349
Left Leg of the Forbidden One	44519536
Legacy Hunter	87010442
Limiter Removal	23171610
Little Chimera	68658728
Luminous Spark	81777047
Luster Dragon	17658803
Luster Dragon #2	11091375
Machine King	46700124
Mad Dog of Darkness	79182538
Mad Sword Beast	79870141
Mage Power	83746708
Magic Cylinder	62279055
Magic Drain	59344077
Magic Swordsman Neo	50930991
Magical Scientist	34206604
Magician of Faith	31560081
Malevolent Nuzzler	99597615
Man Eating Treasure Chest	13723605
Manga Ryu Ran	38369349
Marauding Captain	02460565
Mask Of Darkness	28933734
Mask of Dispel	20765952
Mask of Restrict	29549364
Mask of the Accursed	56948373
Mataza The Zapper	22609617
Mechanicalchaser	07359741
Mega Thunderball	21817254
Melchid the Four-Face Beast	86569121
Metal Guardian	68339286
Millennium Shield	32012841
Milus Radiant	07489323
Mirage Dragon	15960641
Mirror Force	44095762
Mokey Mokey King	13803864
Molten Behemoth	17192817

CARD	PASSWORD
Monster Reborn	83764718
Mother Grizzly	57839750
Mr. Volcano	31477025
Mysterious Guard	01347977
Mystic Plasma Zone	18161786
Mystic Tomato	83011277
Mystic Wok	80161395
Mystical Elf	15025844
Mystical Space Typhoon	05318639
Negate Attack	14315573
Negate Attack	14315573
Ninja Grandmaster Saasuke	04041838
Nobleman of Crossout	71044499
Offerings to the Doomed	19230407
Ooguchi	58861941
Overdrive	02311603
Painful Choice	74191942
Pendulum Machine	24433920
Penguin Soldier	93920745
Peten The Dark Clown	52624755
Pharaoh's Servant	52550973
Pinch Hopper	26185991
Pot of Greed	55144522
Premature Burial	70828912
Princess Of Tsurugi	51371017
Raigeki	12580477
Red-Eyes Black Dragon	74677422
Red-Eyes Black Metal Dragon	64335804
Reflect Bounder	02851070
Reinforcement Of The Army	32807846
Relinquished	64631466
Reload	22589918
Restructer Revolution	99518961
Right Arm of the Forbidden One	70903634
Right Leg of the Forbidden One	08124921
Ring of Destruction	83555666
Robbin' Zombie	83258273
Rogue Doll	91939608
Royal Command	33950246
Rush Recklessly	70046172
Ryu Ran	02964201
Ryu-Kishin Powered	24611934
Sakuretsu Armor	56120475
Seven Tools of the Bandit	03819470

CARD	PASSWORD
Shadow Spell	29267084
Shapesnatch	04035199
Shield To Sword	52097679
Shining Abyss	87303357
Shining Angel	95956346
Shining Friendship	82085619
Silver Fang	90357090
Sinister Serpent	08131171
Skull Dice	00126218
Skull Mariner	05265750
Skull Mark Ladybug	64306248
Skull Servant	32274490
Slate Warrior	78636495
Slot Machine	03797883
Soul of Purity and Light	77527210
Soul Release	05758500
Soul Tiger	15734813
Spear Dragon	31553716
Spell Binding Circle	18807108
Spike Bot	87511987
Spirit Barrier	53239672
Spirit Message "I"	31893528
Spirit Message "L"	30170981
Spirit Message "A"	94772232
Spirit Message "N"	67287533
Spirit of Flames	13522325
St. Joan	21175632
Stray Lambs	60764581
Super Roboyarou	01412158
Susa Soldier	40473581
Sword of Deep-Seated	98495314
Swords of Revealing Light	72302403
Tainted Wisdom	28725004
Takriminos	44073668
Talwar Demon	11761845
The 13th Grave	00032864
The A. Forces	00403847
The All-Seeing White Tiger	32269855
The Bistro Butcher	71107816
The Earl of Demise	66989694
The Forceful Sentry	42829885
The Gross Ghost of Fled Dreams	68049471
The Masked Beast	49064413
The Portrait's Secret	32541773
The Shallow Grave	43434803

CARD	PASSWORD	CARD	PASSWORD
The Unhappy Maiden	51275027	Ultimate Offering	80604091
The Warrior Returning Alive	95281259	United We Stand	56747793
Thousand Eyes Idol	27125110	Unknown Warrior of Fiend	97360116
Thousand Eyes Relinquised	63519819	Ushi Oni	48649353
Time Seal	85316708	Vilepawn Archfiend	73219648
Time Wizard	71625222	Vorse Raider	14898066
Toon Mermaid	65458948	Waboku	12607053
Toon Summoned Skull	91842653	Water Omotics	02483611
Toon World	15259703	Windstorm Of Etaqua	59744639
Tornado Bird	71283180	Wingweaver	31447217
Torrential Tribute	53582587	X-Head Cannon	62651957
Total Defense Shogun	75372290	XY-Dragon cannon	02111707
Trap Hole	04206964	XYZ-Dragon Cannon	91998119
Trap Jammer	19252988	XZ-Tank Cannon	99724761
Tribe Infecting Virus	33184167	Y-Dragon Head	65622692
Tribute to the Doomed	79759861	Yamata Dragon	76862289
Turtle Tiger	37313348	Yata-Garusa	03078576
Two-Headed King Rex	94119974	YZ-Tank Dragon	25119460
UFO Turtle	60806437	Z-Metal Tank	64500000

ZOIDS: LEGACY

CYCLOPES TYPE ONE/TWO, DIABLO TIGER DATA AND ZOID CORES TO BUILD THEM

Complete the game. Then, at the title screen, press L, L, R, R, Up, Down, Up, Down, Left, Left, R, R, Right, Right, Left, Up, Start.

GILVADER, KING GOJULA ZI DATA AND ZOID CORES TO BUILD THEM

Complete the game. Then, at the title screen, press R, R, L, L, Down, Up, Down, Up, Right, Right, L, L, Left, Left, Right, Down, Start.

GAMECUBE™

Contents

1080° AVALANCHE

Select Enter An Avalanche Code from the Options and enter the following codes:

NOVICE AVALANCHE CHALLENGE
Enter JAS3IKRR.

HARD AVALANCHE CHALLENGE
Enter 2AUNIKFS.

EXPERT AVALANCHE CHALLENGE
Enter EATFIKRM.

EXTREME AVALANCHE CHALLENGE
Enter 9AVVIKNY.

ALIEN HOMINID

HATS FOR 2-PLAYER GAME
Go to the Options and rename your alien the following:

abe

april

behemoth

cletus

dandy

goodman

grrl

princess

superfly

BEACH SPIKERS

UNIFORMS
In World Tour, name your player one of the following to unlock bonus outfits. The name disappears when entered correctly.

NAME	UNIFORMS
JUSTICE	105-106, Sunglasses 94
DAYTONA	107-108
FVIPERS	109-110, Face 51, Hair 75
ARAKATA	111-113, Face 52, Hair 76
PHANTA2	114-115, Face 53, Hair 77
OHTORII	116-117

DONKEY KONGA

100M VINE CLIMB (1 OR 2 PLAYERS)
Collect 4800 coins to unlock this mini-game for purchase at DK Town.

BANANA JUGGLE (1 OR 2 PLAYERS)
Collect 5800 coins to unlock this mini-game for purchase at DK Town.

BASH K. ROOL (1 PLAYER)
Collect 5800 coins to unlock this mini-game for purchase at DK Town.

FIFA STREET

ALL APPAREL
At the main menu, hold L + Y and press Right, Right, Left, Up (x3), Down, Left.

MINI PLAYERS
Pause the game, hold L + Y and press Up, Left, Down, Down, Right, Down, Up, Left.

NORMAL SIZE PLAYERS
Pause the game, hold L + Y and press Right, Right, Up, Down, Down, Left, Right, Left.

FUTURE TACTICS: THE UPRISING

UNLIMITED TURNS
During a game, press Up, Up, Down, Down, Left, Right, Left, Left, R, L.

BIG HEADS
During a game, press Up, Left, Down, Left, Down, Up, Up, Left.

DISCO MODE
During a game, press L, Left, L, Left, R, Right, R, Right.

LOW GRAVITY
During a game, press Up (x6), Down, Right, Up.

F-ZERO GX

SOUNDS OF BIG BLUE FOR PURCHASE
Select Customize and enter the shop. Press Z, Left, Right, Left, Z, Y, X, Z, Left, Right, Left, Right, Z, X, Z, X, Z. Select Items to find Sounds of Big Blue for sale.

SOUNDS OF MUTE CITY FOR PURCHASE
Select Customize and enter the shop. Press X (x3), Y, X (x3), Y, Z, Z, Left, Right, Left, Right, Left, Right. Select Items to find Sounds Of Mute City for sale.

RUBY CUP CHAMPIONSHIP

Select Time Attack, then choose Records. Select Ruby Cup, hold L and press R, A, Z, A, C-up, C-Left, A, C-Down, R, Z..

SAPPHIRE CUP CHAMPIONSHIP

Select Time Attack, then choose Records. Select Sapphire Cup, hold Z and press, L, A, L, A, C-Up, L, C-Right, A, R, C-Up.

EMERALD CUP CHAMPIONSHIP

Select Time Attack, then choose Records. Select Emerald Cup, hold R and press Z, A, C-Down, L, C-Left, A, Z, C-Left, L, A.

GOBLIN COMMANDER: UNLEASH THE HORDE

During a game, hold R + L + Y + Down until a message appears in the upper-right corner of the screen. Re-enter the code to disable. Now enter the following codes. Again a message appears if entered correctly.

GOD MODE
Press R (x3), L (x3), R, L, Y, R.

AUTOMATIC WIN
Press R, R, L (x3), R, R, Y (x3).

ALL LEVEL ACCESS
Press Y (x3), L, R, L, L, R, L, R, R, L, R, L, L, R, L, R, L, L, R, L, L, R, L, R, R, Y (x3). Start up a Campaign to select a level.

DISABLE FOG OF WAR
Press R, L, R, R, L, L, Y, Y, L, R.

GAME SPEED X 1/2
Press L (x5), Y (x4), R.

GAME SPEED X 2
Press R (x5), L, Y, R (x3).

GOLD AND SOULS +1000
Press R, R, L, R, R, Y (x3), L, L.

GOLD +100
Press L, R (x4), L, Y, L (x3).

SOULS +100
Press R, L (x4), R, Y, R (x3).

THE HAUNTED MANSION

SKELETON ZEKE
At the legal screen, hold A + B + X + Y. Release at the title screen.

LEVEL SELECT
During a game, hold Right and press X, X, B, Y, Y, B, X, A.

INVINCIBILITY
During a game, hold Right and press B, X (x3), B, X, Y, A.

WEAPON UPGRADE
During a game, hold Right and press B, B, Y, Y, X (x3), A.

THE INCREDIBLES

Pause the game, select Secrets and enter the following codes:

RESTORE SOME HEALTH
Enter **UUDDLRLRBAS**.

BIG HEADS
Enter **EINSTEINIUM**.

SMALL HEADS
Enter **DEEVOLVE**.

ONE HIT KILLS
Enter **KRONOS**.

EYE LASER
Enter **GAZERBEAM**.

WEAKER BOMBS
Enter LABOMBE.

INFINITE INCREDI-POWER FOR ELASTIGIRL
Enter **FLEXIBLE**.

INFINITE INCREDI-POWER FOR MR. INCREDIBLE
Enter **SHOWTIME**.

INFINITE INCREDI-POWER TO MR INCREDIBLE OR ELASTAGIRL
Enter MCTRAVIS.

DESTROYS EVERYTHING
Enter **SMARTBOMB**.

FIRE TRAIL
Enter **ATHLETESFOOT**.

BATTLE MODE
Enter ROTAIDALG.

FASTER GAMEPLAY
Enter **SASSMODE**.

SLOW MOTION
Enter **BWTHEMOVIE**.

DIFFERENT COLORS
Enter DISCORULES.

BRIGHT COLORS
Enter **EMODE**.

INVERT HORIZONTAL CAMERA CONTROL
Enter **INVERTCAMERAX**.

INVERT VERTICAL CAMERA CONTROL
Enter **INVERTCAMERAY**.

TOGGLE HUD
Enter **BHUD**.

WATCH HEAVY IRON STUDIOS INTRO
Enter **HI**.

CREDITS
Enter **YOURNAMEINLIGHTS**.

DEACTIVATE ALL CODES
Enter THEDUDEABIDES.

JIMMY NEUTRON BOY GENIUS

ALL KEY ITEMS
During a game, press R, R, L, A, B, B, A, R, L, R, Start, Down, A, Down.

JIMMY NEUTRON: JET FUSION

ALL MOVIES
During a game, press Z, L, R, R, B, X, X, B, R, R, L, L.
Pause the game, hold L + R and press Up, Up, B, X.

4 HIT COMBO
Pause the game, hold L + R and press A, B, A, Up.

MADDEN NFL 2005

CHEAT CARDS
Select Madden Cards from the My Madden menu. Then, select Madden Codes and enter
the following:

CHEAT	CODE
3rd Down, Opponent only get 3 downs to get a 1st	Z28X8K
5th Down, Get 5 downs to get a 1st Down	P66C4L
Aloha Stadium	G67F5X

CHEAT	CODE
Bingo!, Defensive interceptions increase by 75% for game	J33I8F
Da Bomb, Unlimited pass range	B61A8M
Da Boot, Unlimited field goal range	I76X3T
Extra Credit, Awards points for interceptions and sacks	M89S8G
First and Fifteen, your opponent must get 15 yards to get a 1st down	V65J8P
First and Five, 1st down yards are set to 5	O72E9B
Fumbilitis, Opponents fumbles increase by 75% for game	R14B8Z
Human Plow, Break tackle increases by 75% for game	L96J7P
Lame Duck, Opponent will throw lob passes	D57R5S
Mistake Free, Can't fumble or throw interceptions	X78P9Z
Mr. Mobility, Your QB can't get sacked	Y59R8R
Super Bowl XL	O85P6I
Super Bowl XLI	P48Z4D
Super Bowl XLII	T67R1O
Super Bowl XXXIX	D58F1B
Super Dive, Diving distance increases by 75%	D59K3Y
Tight Fit, Opponents uprights will be narrow	V34L6D
Unforced Errors, Opponent fumble ball when he jukes	L48G1E

CLASSIC TEAM CARDS

Select Madden Cards from the My Madden menu. Then, select Madden Codes and enter the following:

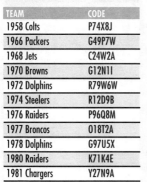

TEAM	CODE
1958 Colts	P74X8J
1966 Packers	G49P7W
1968 Jets	C24W2A
1970 Browns	G12N1I
1972 Dolphins	R79W6W
1974 Steelers	R12D9B
1976 Raiders	P96Q8M
1977 Broncos	O18T2A
1978 Dolphins	G97U5X
1980 Raiders	K71K4E
1981 Chargers	Y27N9A

TEAM	CODE
1982 Redskins	F56D6V
1983 Raiders	D23T8S
1984 Dolphins	X23Z8H
1985 Bears	F92M8M
1986 Giants	K44F2Y
1988 49ers	F77R8H
1990 Eagles	G95F2Q
1991 Lions	I89F4I
1992 Cowboys	I44A1O
1993 Bills	Y66K3O

CHEERLEADER/PUMP UP THE CROWD CARDS

Select Madden Cards from the My Madden menu. Then, select Madden Codes and enter the following:

TEAM	CODE	TEAM	CODE
Patriots	O59P9C	Jaguars	K32C2A
49ers	X61T6L	Jets	S45W1M
Bengals	Y22S6G	Lions	C18F4G
Bills	F26S6X	Packers	K26Y4V
Broncos	B85U5C	Panthers	M66N4D
Browns	B65Q1L	Raiders	G92L2E
Buccaneers	Z55Z7S	Rams	W73B8X
Cardinals	Q91W5L	Ravens	P98T6C
Chargers	Q68S3F	Redskins	N19D6Q
Chiefs	T46M6T	Saints	R99G2F
Colts	M22Z6H	Seahawks	A35T8R
Cowboys	J84E3F	Steelers	C98I2V
Dolphins	E88T2J	Texans	R74G3W
Eagles	Q88P3Q	Titans	Q81V4N
Falcons	W86F3F	Vikings	E26H4L
Giants	L13Z9J		

GOLD PLAYER CARDS

Select Madden Cards from the My Madden menu. Then, select Madden Codes and enter the following:

PLAYER	CODE	PLAYER	CODE
Aaron Brooks	J95K1J	Carson Palmer	O36V2H
Aaron Glenn	Q48E9G	Casey Hampton	Z11P9T
Adewale Ogunleye	C12E9E	Chad Johnson	R85S2A
Ahman Green	T86L4C	Chad Pennington	B64L2F
Al Wilson	G72G2R	Champ Bailey	K89O9E
Alan Faneca	U32S9C	Charles Woodson	F95N9J
Amani Toomer	Z75G6M	Chris Hovan	F14C6J
Andre Carter	V76E2Q	Clinton Portis	Z28D2V
Andre Johnson	E34S1M	Corey Simon	R11D7K
Andy Reid	N44K1L	Courtney Brown	R42R75
Anquan Boldin	S32F7K	Curtis Martin	K47X3G
Antonio Winfield	A12V7Z	Dallas Coach	O24U1Q
Bill Cowher	S54T6U	Damien Woody	E57K9Y
Brad Hopkins	P44A8B	Damien Woody	F78I1I
Bret Farve	L61D7B	Dante Hall	B23P8D
Brian Billick	L27C4K	Dat Nguyen	Q86I2S
Brian Dawkins	Y47B8Y	Daunte Culpepper	O6209K
Brian Simmons	S22M6A	Dave Wannstedt	W73D7D
Brian Urlacher	Z34J4U	David Boston	A25I9F
Brian Westbrook	V46I2I	David Carr	C16E2Q
Bubba Franks	U77F2W	Dennis Erickson	J83E3T
Butch Davis	G77L6F	Dennis Green	C18J7T
Byron Leftwich	C55V5C	Derrick Brooks	P93I9Q

PLAYER	CODE	PLAYER	CODE
Derrick Mason	S98P3T	Keith Brooking	E12P4S
Deuce Mcallister	D11H4J	Keith Bulluck	M63N6V
Dexter Coakley	L35K1A	Kendrell Bell	T96C7J
Dexter Jackson	G16B2I	Kevan Barlow	A23T5E
Dick Vermeil	F68V1W	Kevin Mawee	L76E6S
Dom Capers	B9716R	Kris Jenkins	W63O3K
Domanick Davis	L58S3J	Kyle Boller	A72F9X
Donie Edwards	E18Y5Z	Kyle Turley	Y46A8V
Donovin Darius	Q11T7T	Ladainian Tomlinson	M64D4E
Donovon Mcnabb	T98J11	Lavar Arrington	F19Q8W
Donte Stallworth	R75W3M	Laveranues Coles	R98I5S
Drew Bledsoe	W73M3E	Lawyer Milloy	M37Y5B
Dre'Bly	Z68W8J	La'roi Glover	K24L9K
Dwight Freeney	G76U2L	Lee Suggs	Z94X6Q
Edgerrin James	A75D7X	Leonard Davis	H14M2V
Ed Reed	G18Q2B	Lovie Smith	L38V3A
Eric Moulds	H34Z8K	Marc Bulger	U66B4S
Flozell Adams	R54T1O	Marcel Shipp	R42X2L
Fred Taylor	I87X9Y	Marcus Stroud	E56I5O
Grant Wistrom	E46M4Y	Marcus Trufant	R46T5U
Herman Edwards	O19T2T	Mark Brunell	B66D9J
Hines Ward	M12B8F	Marshell Faulk	U76G1U
Jack Del Rio	J22P9I	Marty Booker	P51U4B
Jake Delhomme	M86N9F	Marty Booker	H19Q2O
Jake Plummer	N74P8X	Marty Shottenheimer	D96A7S
Jamie Sharper	W27I7G	Marvin Harrison	T11E8O
Jason Taylor	O33S6I	Marvin Lewis	P24S4H
Jason Webster	M74B3E	Matt Hasselback	R68D5F
Jeff Fisher	N62B6J	Michael Bennett	W81W2J
Jeff Garcia	H32H7B	Michael Strahan	O66T6K
Jeremy Newberry	J77Y8C	Michael Vick	H67B1F
Jeremy Shockey	R34X5T	Mike Alstott	D89F6W
Jerry Porter	F71Q9Z	Mike Brown	F12J8N
Jerry Rice	K34F8S	Mike Martz	R64A8E
Jevon Kearse	A78B1C	Mike Mularkey	C56D6E
Jim Haslett	G78R3W	Mike Rucker	K89O6S
Jim Mora Jr.	N46C3M	Mike Shanahan	H15L5Y
Jimmy Smith	I22J5W	Mike Sherman	F84X6K
Joe Horn	P91A1Q	Mike Tice	Y31T6Y
John Fox	Q98R7Y	New England Coach	N24L4Z
Jon Gruden	H61I8A	Nick Bernett	X95I7S
Josh Mccown	O33Y4X	Norv Turner	F24K1M
Julian Peterson	M89J8A	Olin Kreutz	R17R2O
Julius Peppers	X54O4Z	Orlando Pace	U42U9U
Junior Seau	W26K6Q	Patrick Surtain	H58T9X
Kabeer Gbaja-Biamala	U16I9Y	Peerless Price	X75V6K

PLAYER	CODE	PLAYER	CODE
Peter Warrick	D86P80	Simeon Rice	S62F9T
Peyton Manning	L48H4U	Stephen Davis	E39X9L
Plaxico Burress	K18P6J	Steve Mariucci	V74Q3N
Priest Holmes	X91N1L	Steve Mcnair	S36T1I
Quentin Jammer	V55S3Q	Steve Smith	W91O2O
Randy Moss	W79U7X	T.J. Duckett	P67E1I
Ray Lewis	B94X6V	Takeo Spikes	B83A6C
Reggie Wayne	R29S8C	Tedy Bruschi	K28Q3P
Rex Grossman	C46P2A	Terence Newman	W57Y5P
Rich Gannon	Q69I1Y	Terrell Suggs	V71A9Q
Richard Seymore	L69T4T	Tiki Barber	T43A2V
Ricky Williams	P19V1N	Todd Heap	H19M1G
Rod Smith	V22C4L	Tom Brady	X22V7E
Rodney Harrison	O84I3J	Tom Coughlin	S71D6H
Rondel Barber	J72X8W	Tony Dungy	Y96R8V
Roy Williams	J76C6F	Tony Gonzalez	N46E9N
Rudi Johnson	W26J6H	Torry Holt	W96U7E
Sam Madison	Z87T5C	Travis Henry	F36M2Q
Samari Rolle	C69H4Z	Trent Green	Y46M4S
Santana Moss	H79E5B	Ty Law	F13W1Z
Seattle Coach	V58U4Y	Walter Jones	G57P1P
Shaun Alexander	C95Z4P	Washington Coach	W63V9L
Shaun Ellis	Z54F2B	Will Shields	B52S8A
Shaun Rogers	J97X8M	Zach Thomas	U63I3H
Shawn Springs	J95K1J		

MARIO GOLF: TOADSTOOL TOUR

At the title screen, press Start + Z to open the password screen. Enter the following to open up bonus tournaments:

TARGET BULLSEYE TOURNAMENT
Enter CEUFPXJ1.

HOLLYWOOD VIDEO TOURNAMENT
Enter BJGQBULZ.

CAMP HYRULE TOURNAMENT
Enter 0EKW5G7U.

BOWSER BADLANDS TOURNAMENT
Enter 9L3L9KHR.

BOWSER JR.'S JUMBO TOURNAMENT
Enter 2GPL67PN.

MARIO OPEN TOURNAMENT
Enter GGAA241H.

PEACH'S INVITATIONAL TOURNAMENT
Enter ELBUT3PX.

MARIO POWER TENNIS

EVENT GAMES
At the title screen, hold Z and press Start.

MVP BASEBALL 2005

ALL STADIUMS, PLAYERS, UNIFORMS AND REWARDS
Create a player named Katie Roy.

RED SOX ST. PATRICK'S DAY UNIFORM
Create a player named Neverlose Sight.

BAD HITTER WITH THIN BAT
Create a player named Erik Kiss.

GOOD HITTER WITH BIG BAT
Create a player named Isaiah Paterson, Jacob Paterson or Keegan Paterson.

BIGGER BODY
Create a player named Kenny Lee.

NASCAR 2005: CHASE FOR THE CUP

ALL BONUSES
At the Edit Driver screen, enter Open Sesame as your name.

DALE EARNHARDT
At the Edit Driver screen, enter The Intimidator as your name.

$10,000,000

At the Edit Driver screen, enter Walmart NASCAR as your name.

LAKESHORE DRIVE TRACK

At the Edit Driver screen, enter Walmart Exclusive as your name.

DODGE EVENTS

At the Edit Driver screen, enter Dodge Stadium as your name.

MR CLEAN DRIVERS

At the Edit Driver screen, enter Mr.Clean Racing as your name.

MR. CLEAN PIT CREW

At the Edit Driver screen, enter Clean Crew as your name.

2,000,000 PRESTIGE POINTS/LEVEL 10 IN FIGHT TO THE TOP MODE
At the Edit Driver screen, enter You TheMan as your name.

NBA LIVE 2004

Create a player with the following last name. The player will be placed in Free Agents.

ALEKSANDER PAVLOVIC
Enter WHSUCPOI.

ANDREAS GLYNIADAKIS
Enter POCKDLEK.

CARLOS DELFINO
Enter SDFGURKL.

JAMES LANG
Enter NBVKSMCN.

JERMAINE DUPRI
Enter SOSODEF.

KYLE KORVER
Enter OEISNDLA.

MALICK BADIANE
Enter SKENXIDO.

MARIO AUSTIN
Enter POSNEGHX.

MATT BONNER
Enter BBVDKCVM.

NEDZAD SINANOVIC
Enter ZXDSDRKE.

PACCELIS MORLENDE
Enter QWPOASZX.

REMON VAN DE HARE
Enter ITNVCJSD.

RICK RICKERT
Enter POILKJMN.

SANI BECIROVIC
Enter ZXCCVDRI.

SOFOKLIS SCHORTSANITIS
Enter IOUBFDCJ.

SZYMON SZEWCZYK
Enter POIOIJIS.

TOMMY SMITH
Enter XCFWQASE.

XUE YUYANG
Enter WMZKCOI.

Select NBA Codes from the My NBA LIVE option and enter the following

15,000 NBA STORE POINTS
Enter 87843H5F9P.

ALL HARDWOOD CLASSIC JERSEYS
Enter 725JKUPLMM.

ALL NBA GEAR
Enter ERT9976KJ3.

ALL TEAM GEAR
Enter YREY5625WQ.

ALL SHOES
Enter POUY985GY5.

UNLOCK SHOES

SHOES

Select My NBA Live and enter the following NBA Codes to unlock the different shoes

SHOES	CODE
Air Bounds (black/white/blue)	7YSS0292KE
Air Bounds (white/black)	JA807YAM20
Air Bounds (white/green)	84HHST61QI
Air Flight 89 (black/white)	FG874JND84
Air Flight 89 (white/black)	63RBVC7423
Air Flight 89 (white/red)	GF9845JHR4
Air Flightposite 2 (blue/gray)	2389JASE3E
Air Flightposite (white/black/gray)	74FDH7K94S
Air Flightposite (white/black)	6HJ874SFJ7
Air Flightposite (yellow/black/white)	MN54BV45C2
Air Flightposite 2 (blue/gray)	RB84UJHAS2
Air Flightposite 2 (blue/gray)	2389JASE3E
Air Foamposite 1 (blue)	OP5465UX12
Air Foamposite 1 (white/black/red)	D0D843HH7F
Air Foamposite Pro (blue/black)	DG56TRF446
Air Foamposite Pro (black/gray)	3245AFSD45
Air Foamposite Pro (red/black)	DSAKF38422
Air Force Max (black)	F84N845H92
Air Force Max (white/black/blue)	985KJF98KJ
Air Force Max (white/red)	8734HU8FFF
Air Hyperflight (white)	14TGU7DEWC
Air Hyperflight (black/white)	WW44YHU592
Air Hyperflight (blue/white)	AOK374HF8S
Air Hyperflight (yellow/black)	JCX93LSS88
Air Jordan 11 (black/red/white)	GF64H76ZX5
Air Jordan 11 (black/varsity royal/white)	HJ987RTGFA

SHOES	CODE
Air Jordan 11 (cool grey)	GF75HG6332
Air Jordan 11 (white)	HG76HN765S
Air Jordan 11 (white/black)	A2S35TH7H6
Air Jordan 3 (white)	G9845HJ8F4
Air Jordan 3 (white/clay)	435SGF555Y
Air Jordan 3 (white/fire red)	RE6556TT90
Air Jordan 3 (white/true blue)	FDS9D74J4F
Air Jordan 3 (black/white/gray)	CVJ554TJ58
Air Max2 CB (black/white)	87HZXGFIU8
Air Max2 CB (white/red)	4545GFKJIU
Air Max2 Uptempo (black/white/blue)	NF8745J87F
Air Max Elite (black)	A4CD54T7TD
Air Max Elite (white/black)	966ERTFG65
Air Max Elite (white/blue)	FD9KN48FJF
Air Zoom Flight (gray/white)	367UEY6SN
Air Zoom Flight (white/blue)	92387HDO77
Zoom Generation (white/black/red)	23LBJNUMB1
Zoom Generation (black/red/white)	LBJ23CAVS1
Nike Blazer (khaki)	W3R57U9NB2
Nike Blazer (tan/white/blue)	DCT5YHMU90
Nike Blazer (white/orange/blue)	4G66JU99XS
Nike Blazer (black)	XCV6456NNL
Nike Shox BB4 (black)	WE424TY563
Nike Shox BB4 (white/black)	23ERT85LP9
Nike Shox BB4 (white/light purple)	668YYTRB12
Nike Shox BB4 (white/red)	424TREU777
Nike Shox VCIII (black)	SDFH764FJU
Nike Shox VCIII (white/black/red)	5JHD367JJT

NBA STREET VOL. 2

Select Pick Up Game, hold L and enter the following when "Enter cheat codes now" appears at the bottom of the screen:

UNLIMITED TURBO
Press B, B, Y, Y.

ABA BALL
Press X, B, X, B.

WNBA BALL
Press X, Y, Y, X.

NO DISPLAY BARS
Press B, X (x3).

ALL JERSEYS
Press X, Y, B, B.

ALL COURTS
Press B, Y, Y, B.

ST. LUNATICS TEAM AND ALL STREET LEGENDS
Press X, Y, B, Y.

ALL NBA LEGENDS
Press X, Y, Y, B.

CLASSIC MICHAEL JORDAN
Press X, Y, X, X.

EXPLOSIVE RIMS
Press X (x3), Y.

SMALL PLAYERS
Press Y, Y, X, B.

BIG HEADS
Press X, B, B, X.

ALL QUICKS
Press Y, X, Y, B.

NO COUNTERS
Press Y, Y, X, X.

EASY SHOTS
Press Y, X, B, Y.

BALL TRAILS
Press Y, Y, Y, B.

HARD SHOTS
Press Y, B, X, Y.

NCAA FOOTBALL 2005

PENNANT CODES
Select My NCAA and then Pennant Collection. Enter the following Pennant Codes:

CODE	EFFECT
EA Sports	Cuffed Cheat
Thanks	1st and 15
Sic Em	Baylor powerup
For	Blink (ball spotted short)
Registering	Boing (dropped passes)
Tiburon	Crossed The Line
Oskee Wow	Illinois Team Boost
Hike	Jumbalaya
Home Field	Molasses Cheat
Elite 11	QB Dud
NCAA	Stiffed
Football	Take Your Time
Fight	Texas Tech Team Boost
2005	Thread The Needle
Tech Triumph	Virginia Tech Team Boost
Blitz	What a Hit
Fumble	2003 All-Americans
Roll Tide	Alabama All-time
Raising Cane	Miami All-time
Go Blue	Michigan All-time
Hail State	Mississippi State All-time
Go Big Red	Nebraska All-time
Rah Rah	North Carolina All-time
We Are	Penn State All-time

CODE	EFFECT
Death Valley	Clemson All-time
Glory	Colorado All-time
Victory	Kansas State All-time
Quack Attack	Oregon All-time
Fight On	USC All-time
Bow Down	Washington All-time
Bear Down	Arizona mascot team
WooPigSooie	Arkansas All-time
War Eagle	Auburn All-time
U Rah Rah	Badgers All-time
Great To Be	Florida All-time
Great To Be	Florida All-time
Uprising	Florida State All-time
Hunker Down	Georgia All-time
On Iowa	Iowa All-time
Geaux Tigers	LSU All-time
Golden Domer	Notre Dame All-time
Boomer	Oklahoma All-time
Go Pokes	Oklahoma State All-time
Lets Go Pitt	Pittsburgh All-time
Boiler Up	Purdue All-time
Orange Crush	Syracuse All-time
Big Orange	Tennessee All-time
Gig Em	Texas A&M All-time
Hook Em	Texas All-time
Mighty	UCLA All-time
Killer Bucks	Ohio State All-time
Killer Nuts	Ohio State All-time
Wahoos	Virginia All-time
Ramblinwreck	Georgia Tech Mascot Team
Red And Gold	Iowa St. Mascot Team
Rock Chalk	Kansas Mascot Team
On On UK	Kentucky Mascot Team
Go Green	Michigan State Mascot Team
Rah Rah Rah	Minnesota Mascot Team
Mizzou Rah	Missouri Mascot Team
Go Pack	NC State Mascot Team
Go Cats	NU Mascot Team
Hotty Totty	Ole Miss Mascot Team
Hail WV	West Virginia Mascot Team
Go Deacs Go	Wake Forest Mascot Team
All Hail	WSU Mascot Team

NEED FOR SPEED UNDERGROUND 2

$200 IN CAREER MODE
At the title screen, press Up, Up, Up, Left, R, R, R, Down.

$1000 IN CAREER MODE
At the title screen, press Left, Left, Right, X, X, Right, L, R.

HUMMER H2 CAPONE
At the title screen, press Up, Left, Up, Up, Down, Left, Down, Left.

LEXUS IS300
At the title screen, press Up, Down, Left, Up, Left, Up, Right, Left.

BEST BUY VINYL
At the title screen, press Up, Down, Up, Down, Down, Up, Right, Left.

BURGER KING VINYL
At the title screen, press Up, Up, Up, Up, Down, Up, Up, Left.

PERFORMANCE LEVEL 1
At the title screen, press L, R, L, R, Left, Left, Right, Up.

PERFORMANCE LEVEL 2
At the title screen, press R, R, L, R, Left, Right, Up, Down.

VISUAL LEVEL 1
At the title screen, press R, R, Up, Down, L, L, Up, Down.

VISUAL LEVEL 2
At the title screen, press L, R, Up, Down, L, Up, Up, Down.

NFL STREET 2

Select Cheats from the Options and enter the following:

FUMBLE MODE
Enter GreasedPig as a code.

MAX CATCHING
Enter MagnetHands as a code.

NO FIRST DOWNS
Enter NoChains as a code.

NO FUMBLES MODE
Enter GlueHands as a code.

UNLIMITED TURBO
Enter NozBoost as a code.

EA FIELD
Enter EAField as a code.

GRIDIRON PARK
Enter GRIDIRONPRK as a code.

AFC EAST ALL STARS
Enter EAASFSCT as a code.

AFC NORTH ALL STARS
Enter NAOFRCTH as a code.

AFC SOUTH ALL STARS
Enter SAOFUCTH as a code.

AFC WEST ALL STARS
Enter WAEFSCT as a code.

NFC EAST ALL STARS
Enter NNOFRCTH as a code.

NFC NORTH ALL STARS
Enter NNAS66784 as a code.

NFC SOUTH ALL STARS
Enter SNOFUCTH as a code.

NFC WEST ALL STARS
Enter ENASFSCT as a code.

REEBOK TEAM
Enter Reebo as a code.k

TEAM XZIBIT
Enter TeamXzibit as a code.

PIKMIN 2

TITLE SCREEN
At the title screen, use the following controls:
Press R to make the Pikmin form NINTENDO.
Press L to go back to PIKMIN 2.

Press X to get a beetle.
Use the C-Stick to move it around.
Press L to get rid of the Beetle.

Press Y to get a Chappie.
Use the C-Stick to move it around.
Press Z to eat the Pikmin.
Press L to get rid of Chappie.

RAVE MASTER

REINA
At the title screen press Up, Up, Down, Down, Left, Right, Left, Right, B, A.

ROBOTS

BIG HEAD
Pause the game and press Up, Down, Down, Up, Right, Right, Left, Right.

INVINCIBLE
Pause the game and press Up, Right, Down, Up, Left, Down, Right, Left.

UNLIMITED SCRAP
Pause the game and press Down, Down, Left, Up, Up, Right, Up, Down.

THE SIMS: BUSTIN' OUT

Pause the game, then enter the following codes. You must enter the Enable Cheats code first. After entering another code, select the gnome to access it.

ENABLE CHEATS
Press Down, L, Z, R, Left, X. A gnome appears in front of your house when the code is entered correctly.

FILL ALL MOTIVES
Press L, R, Y, Down, Down, X.

UNLOCK ALL LOCATIONS
Press Down, Z, R, L, Z.

UNLOCK ALL OBJECTS
Press Down, Z, Up, Y, R.

UNLOCK ALL SKINS
Press L, Y, A, R, Left.

UNLOCK ALL SOCIAL OPTIONS
Press L, R, Down, Down, Y.

SONIC HEROES

METAL CHARACTERS IN 2-PLAYER
After selecting a level in 2-Player, hold A + Y.

SPIDER-MAN 2

TREYARCH PASSWORD
Start a New Game and enter HCRAYERT as your name. You will start at 44% complete, 201, 000 Hero Points, some upgrades and more.

SSX 3

Select Options from the Main Menu. Choose Cheat Codes from the Options menu and enter the following codes to unlock each character. To access the characters, go to the Lodge and select Rider Details. Then select Cheat Characters to find them.

BRODI
Enter zenmaster.

BUNNY SAN
Enter wheresyourtail.

CANHUCK
Enter greatwhitenorth.

CHURCHILL
Enter tankengine.

CUDMORE
Enter milkemdaisy.

EDDIE
Enter worm.

GUTLESS
Enter boneyardreject.

HIRO
Enter slicksuit.

JJ
Enter potty.

JURGEN
Enter brokenleg.

LUTHER
Enter bronco.

MARTY
Enter back2future.

NORTH WEST LEGEND
Enter callhimgeorge.

SNOWBALLS
Enter betyouveneverseen.

STRETCH
Enter windmilldunk.

SVELTE LUTHER
Enter notsosvelte.

UNKNOWN RIDER
Enter finallymadeitin.

PEAK 1 CLOTHES
Enter shoppingspree.

ALL PEAKS
Enter biggerthank7.

ALL ARTWORK
Enter naturalconcept.

ALL BOARDS
Enter graphicdelight.

ALL VIDEOS
Enter myeyesaredim.

ALL PLAYLIST SONGS
Enter djsuperstar.

ALL TOYS
Enter nogluerequired.

ALL TRADING CARDS
Enter gotitgotitneedit.

ALL POSTERS
Enter postnobills.

STAR WARS ROGUE SQUADRON III: REBEL STRIKE

Select Passcodes from the Options and enter the following. When there are two passcodes, enter the first and Enter Code. Then enter the second and Enter Code.

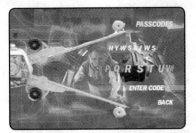

UNLIMITED LIVES
Enter IIOUAOYE, then enter WIMPIAM!.

ACE MODE
Enter YNMSFY?P, then enter YOUDAMAN.

LEVEL SELECT IN COOPERATIVE MODE
Enter SWGRCQPL, then enter UCHEATED.

ALL SINGLE PLAYER MISSIONS
Enter HYWSC!WS, then enter NONGAMER.

ALL SINGLE PLAYER MISSIONS PLUS BONUS MISSIONS
Enter EEQQ?YPL, then enter CHE!ATER.

BEGGAR'S CANYON RACE IN COOPERATIVE
Enter FRLL!CSF, then enter FARMBOY?.

ASTEROID FIELD MISSION IN COOPERATIVE
Enter RWALPIGC, then enter NOWAYOUT.

DEATH STAR ESCAPE MISSION IN COOPERATIVE
Enter YFCEDFRH, then enter DSAGAIN?.

ENDURANCE MISSION IN COOPERATIVE
Enter WPX?FGC!, then enter EXCERSIZ.

ALL SHIPS IN VERSUS
Enter W!WSTPQB, then enter FREEPLAY.

MILLENNIUM FALCON
Enter QZCRPTG!, then enter HANSRIDE.

NABOO STARFIGHTER
Enter RTWCVBSH, then enter BFNAGAIN.

SLAVE I
Enter TGBCWLPN, then enter ZZBOUNTY.

TIE BOMBER
Enter JASDJWFA, then enter !DABOMB!.

TIE HUNTER
Enter FRRVBMJK, then enter LOOKOUT!.

TIE FIGHTER IN COOPERATIVE
Enter MCKEMAKD, then enter ONESHOT!.

TIE ADVANCE IN COOPERATIVE
Enter VDX?WK!H, then enter ANOKSHIP.

RUDY'S CAR
Enter AXCBPRHK, then enter WHATTHE?.

CREDITS
Enter LOOKMOM!. Find this in the Special Features menu.

STAR WARS ARCADE GAME
Enter RTJPFC!G, then enter TIMEWARP.

EMPIRE STRIKES BACK ARCADE GAME
Enter !H!F?HXS, then enter KOOLSTUF.

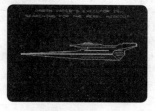

DOCUMENTARY
Enter THEDUDES.

ART GALLERY
Enter !KOOLART.

MUSIC HALL
Enter HARKHARK.

BLACK AND WHITE
Enter NOCOLOR?.

TEENAGE MUTANT NINJA TURTLES 2: BATTLE NEXUS

Select Password from the Options menu and enter the following. Hold L while selecting a turtle to get his New Nexus Turtle outfit.

EFFECT	PASSWORD
Challenge Code Abyss	SDSDRLD
Challenge Code Endurance	MRMDRMD
Challenge Code Fatal Blow	LRSRDRD
Challenge Code Lose Shuriken	RLMRDSL
Challenge Code Nightmare	SLSDRDL
Challenge Code Poison	DRSLLSR
Challenge Code Super-Tough	RDSRMRL
Cheat Code All-You-Can-Throw Shuriken	RSRLRSM
Cheat Code Health	DSRDMRM
Cheat Code Mighty Turtle	LSDRRDR
Cheat Code Pizza Paradise	MRLMRMR
Cheat Code Self Recovery	DRMSRLR
Cheat Code Squeaking	MLDSRDM
Cheat Code Super Defense Power	LDRMRLM

EFFECT	PASSWORD
Cheat Code Super Offense Power	SDLSRLL
Cheat Code Toddling	SSSMRDD
New Nexus Turtle outfit for Donatello	DSLRDRM
New Nexus Turtle outfit for Leonardo	LMRMDRD
New Nexus Turtle outfit for Michelangelo	MLMRDRM
New Nexus Turtle outfit for Raphael	RMSRMDR
Playmates added to Bonus Materials	SRMLDDR

TIGER WOODS PGA TOUR 2004

ALL GOLFERS AND COURSES
Enter THEKITCHENSINK.

ALL GOLFERS
Enter CANYOUPICKONE

ALL COURSES
Enter ALLTHETRACKS.

TARGET SHOOTOUT
Enter sherwood target.

ACE ANDREWS
Enter ACEINTHEHOLE.

CEDRIC THE ENTERTAINER
Enter CEDDYBEAR.

DOMINIC "THE DON" DONATELLO
Enter DISCOKING.

DOWNTOWN BROWN
Enter DTBROWN.

EDWIN "POPS" MASTERSON
Enter EDDIE.

ERICA ICE
Enter ICYONE.

HAMISH "MULLIGAN" MEGREGOR
Enter DWILBY.

MOA "BIG MO" TA'A VATU
Enter ERUPTION.

SOLITA LOPEZ
Enter SHORTGAME.

SUNDAY TIGER
Enter 4REDSHIRTS.

TAKEHARU "TSUNAMI" MOTO
Enter EMERALDCHAMP.

VAL SUMMERS
Enter BEVERLYHILLS.

"YOSH" TANIGAWA
Enter THENEWLEFTY.

TIGER WOODS PGA TOUR 2005

Select Passwords and enter the following:

ALL GOLFERS AND COURSES
Enter THEGIANTOYSTER.

ALL COURSES
Enter THEWORLDISYOURS

THE CITY ROOFTOPS SKILL ZONE
Enter NIGHTGOLFER.

ADIDAS ITEMS
Enter 91treSTR

CALLAWAY ITEMS
Enter cgTR78qw

CLEVELAND ITEMS
Enter CL45etUB

MAXFLI ITEMS
Enter FDGH597i

NIKE ITEMS
Enter YJHk342B

ODYSSEY ITEMS
Enter kjnMR3qv

PING ITEMS
Enter R453DrTe

PRECEPT ITEMS
Enter BRi3498Z

TAG ITEMS
Enter cDsa2fgY

TOURSTAGE ITEMS
Enter TS345329

TIFFANY WILLIAMSON
Enter RICHGIRL

JEB "SHOOTER" MCGRAW
Enter SIXSHOOTER

HUNTER "STEELHEAD" ELMORE
Enter GREENCOLLAR

ALASTAIR" CAPTAIN" MCFADDEN
Enter NICESOCKS

BEV "BOOMER" BUOUCHIER
Enter THEBEEHIVE

ADRIANA "SUGAR" DULCE
Enter SOSWEET

APHRODITE PAPADAPOLUS
Enter TEMPTING

BILLY "BEAR" HIGHTOWER
Enter TOOTALL

KENDRA "SPIKE" LOVETTE
Enter ENGLISHPUNK

DION "DOUBLE D" DOUGLAS
Enter DDDOUGLAS

RAQUEL "ROCKY" ROGERS
Enter DOUBLER

BUNJIRO "BUD" TANAKA
Enter INTHEFAMILY

CEASAR "THE EMPEROR" ROSADO
Enter LANDOWNER

REGINALD WEATHERS
Enter REGGIE

THE HUSTLER
Enter ALTEREGO

SUNDAY TIGER WOODS
Enter NEWLEGEND

SEVE BALLESTEROS
Enter THEMAGICIAN

BEN HOGAN
Enter PUREGOLF

JACK NICKLAUS
Enter GOLDENBEAR.

ARNOLD PALMER
Enter THEKING.

GARY PLAYER
Enter BLACKKNIGHT.

JUSTIN TIMBERLAKE
Enter THETENNESSEEKID.

TONY HAWK'S UNDERGROUND

Select Cheat Codes from the options and enter the following. Some cheats will need to be turned on by pausing the game and selecting Cheats from the Options menu.

PLAY AS T.H.U.D.
Enter NOOO!!.

PERFECT RAIL
Enter letitslide.

PERFECT SKITCH
Enter rearrider.

PERFECT MANUAL
Enter keepitsteady.

MOON GRAVITY
Enter getitup.

TONY HAWK'S UNDERGROUND 2

ALWAYS SPECIAL

Select Cheat Codes from the Game Options and enter likepaulie. Select Cheats from the Game Options to toggle on and off.

PERFECT RAIL

Select Cheat Codes from the Game Options and enter straightedge. Select Cheats from the Game Options to toggle on and off.

TY THE TASMANIAN TIGER 2: BUSH RESCUE

ALL BUNYIP KEYS
During a game, press Start, Y, Start, Start, Y, B, X, B, A.

ALL FIRST-LEVEL RANGS
During a game, press Start, Y, Start, Start, Y, X, B, X, B.

ALL SECOND-LEVEL RANGS
During a game, press Start, Y, Start, Start, Y, B, X, B, Y.

GET 100,000 OPALS
During a game, press Start, Y, Start, Start, Y, X, A, X, A.

HIGHLIGHT ALL COLLECTIBLES
During a game, press Start, Y, Start, Start, Y, Up, Down, Left, Right.

THE URBZ: SIMS IN THE CITY

CHEAT GNOME
During a game, press Down + L + Z + R + X + Left. Now you can enter the following cheats.

MAX ARTISTIC
Press R, Y, Up Z, Down.

MAX MENTAL
Press Down, X, Left, R, Down.

MAX PHYSTICAL
Press R, Z, Down, Y, Y.

ACQUIRE SKILL
Press Down, Z, Up, Y, R.

POWER SOCIAL
Press B, Left, X, R, L, A.

TEAM PHOTO
At the credits screen, press Up, Down, A, Up, Down, A.

X2: WOLVERINE'S REVENGE

ALL MOVIES
At the main menu, press B, X, B, Y, Y, Y, R, R, Z.

XGRA: EXTREME-G RACING ASSOCIATION

ALL LEVELS OF RACING
Enter FREEPLAY at the Cheat Menu.

ALL TRACKS
Enter WIBBLE at the Cheat Menu.

O2 LIVERIED
Enter UCANDO at the Cheat Menu.

MESSAGE IN CREDITS
Enter MUNCHKIN, EDDROOLZ or EDDIEPOO at the Cheat Menu.

YU-GI-OH: FALSEBOUND KINGDOM

GOLD COINS
On an empty piece of land, during a mission, press Up, Up, Down, Down, Left, Right, Left, Right, B, A.

NINTENDO DS™

The Games

ASPHALT URBAN GT

MONEY FOR NOTHING
Buy the Chevrolet 2005 Corvette C6 for $45,000. Then, go to your garage and sell it for $45,500.

FEEL THE MAGIC: XY/XX

HARD MODE
Defeat the game on Normal difficulty.

HELL MODE
Defeat the game on Hard difficulty.

PING PALS

50 COINS
Select Credits and let them run to the end.

HOLIDAY ITEMS
Set the date on your Nintendo DS to the following dates to get access to special Holiday Items:

DATE	ITEM	COST
February 14	Valentine (Boy)	300 Coins
February 14	Valentine (Girl)	200 Coins
February 21	Vessel Top	700 Coins
March 17	Snowflake	250 Coins
October 31	Bat Treats	400 Coins
October 31	Jack Hat	4000 Coins
October 31	Succubus	321 Coins
December 25	Elf Skirt	300 Coins
December 25	Jolly Suit	300 Coins
December 25	Merry Cap	10 Coins

DATE	ITEM	COST
Birthday	Birthday (Boy)	5 Coins
Birthday	Birthday (Girl)	5 Coins

SHANTAE BACKGROUND
Touch the Ping Pals logo exactly at midnight.

PUYO POP FEVER

ALL CHARACTERS AND CUTSCENES
Select Gallery from the Options. Highlight cutscene viewer, hold X and press Up, Down, Left, Right.

RIDGE RACER DS

UNLOCK CARS
Race more than ten multi-player races to unlock the following cars: 00-Agent Car, Caddy Car, Galaga '88, Mario Racing, Pooka, Red Shirt Rage, Shy Guy.

DS CAR
Defeat Ridge Racer Extreme in Extra Mode.

SPIDER-MAN 2

ALL SPECIAL MOVES
Load the game with Spider-Man: Mysterio's Menace for Game Boy Advance in the Nintendo DS.

TIGER WOODS PGA TOUR

EMERALD DRAGON
Earn $1,000,000.

GREEK ISLES
Earn $1,500,000.

PARADISE COVER
Earn $2,000,000.

EA SPORTS FAVORITES
Earn $5,000,000

MEAN8TEEN
Earn $10,000,000.

FANTASY SPECIALS
Earn $15,000,000.

LEGEND COMPILATION 1
Defeat Hogan in Legend Tour.

LEGEND COMPILATION 2
Defeat Gary Player in Legend Tour.

LEGEND COMPILATION 3
Defeat Ballesteros in Legend Tour.

LEGEND COMPILATION 4
Defeat Palmer in Legend Tour.

LEGEND COMPILATION 5
Defeat Nicklaus in Legend Tour.

THE HUSTLER'S DREAM 18
Defeat The Hustler in Legend Tour.

TIGER'S DREAM 18
Defeat Tiger Woods in Legend Tour.

THE URBZ: SIMS IN THE CITY

CLUB XIZZLE
Once you gain access to Club Xizzle, enter with the password "bucket."

PLAYSTATION®

The Games

ACTION MAN: MISSION XTREME

ALL TOOLS AND WEAPONS
Pause the game and press 🔲, 🔲, 🔲.

INVINCIBILITY
Pause the game and press 🔲, 🔲, 🔲.

ARMY MEN: WORLD WAR FINAL FRONT

ALL WEAPONS
Pause the game, hold 🔲 + 🔲, and press ✖ , ⬤, Up, Up, ⬤, Down.

C-12: FINAL RESISTANCE

INVINCIBLE
Pause the game, hold ⬛, and press Up, Left, Down, Right, ▲, ■, ✖, ●.

ALL WEAPONS
Pause the game, hold ⬛, and press Up, Left, Right, Down, ▲, ■, ●, ✖.

SHIELD
Pause the game, hold ⬛, and press Up, Left, Right, ▲, ■, ●.

INFINITE AMMO
Pause the game, hold ⬛, and press Down, Left, Right, ✖, ■, ●.

SECONDARY WEAPON ATTACKS
Pause the game, hold ⬛, and press Up, Down, Left, Right, ▲, ✖, ■, ●.

STEALTH MODE
Pause the game, hold ⬛, and press ✖, ✖, ■, ■, ▲, ▲, ●, ●, ✖, ✖.

DELTA FORCE: URBAN WARFARE

CHEAT MENU
At the main menu, press Select, Right, Up, Down, ●, Left, ■, ▲, ●.

FINAL FANTASY ORIGINS

FINAL FANTASY

THE TILE GAME
When you're on your ship, hold ✖, then press ● 55 times to bring up a sliding tile puzzle game called 15 Puzzle. The game tracks your best time and rewards you accordingly:

Under 6 Minutes: Potion

Under 4 Minutes: Antidote and Potion

Under 2 Minutes: Golden Needle, Antidote, and Potion

1st Place Finish: 10,000 Gil

2nd Place Finish: 5,000 Gil

3rd Place Finish: 2,000 Gil

FINAL FANTASY 2

CONCENTRATION MINI GAME
After you obtain the Snowcraft, hold ✖ and press ● 15-20 times to start a game of concentration. An easy way to earn the maximum reward of 40,000 Gil, an Elixir, and a Phoenix Down, is to beat the first puzzle and note the locations of the pairs. Restart and quit the game 31 times. (Don't exit the game screen; just cancel immediately after starting a game.) Then, the thirty-second layout is the same as the first board.

HOT SHOTS GOLF 2

ALL CHARACTERS
Enter 2gsh as your name.

THE ITALIAN JOB

Enter the following at the main menu, unless otherwise noted. Applause will indicate correct entry.

ALL CHEATS
Press ▲, ⊙, ▲, ⊙, ▲, ■, ▲, ■

ALL MISSIONS IN ITALIAN JOB MODE
Press ⊙, ⊙, ▲, ■, ■.

ALL MISSIONS IN CHALLENGE MODE
Press ■, ■, ▲, ⊙, ⊙, ■, ▲, ⊙.

ALL MISSIONS IN CHECKPOINT MODE
Press ⊙, ■, ▲, ■, ▲, ■, ▲, ■, ⊙.

ALL MISSIONS IN DESTRUCTOR MODE
Press ▲, ■, ■, ▲, ■, ▲, ■, ⊙ (3).

ALL MISSIONS IN FREE RIDE
Press ■, ▲, ■, ⊙ (3), ▲, ⊙.

LEVEL SELECT
In Career mode, pause the game, hold ▥, and press ▲, Left, Left, ▲, ⊙, Up, Up, ■.

MAT HOFFMAN'S PRO BMX

During a session in a level, press Start. At the Pause menu, hold ▥ and enter the following codes:

8 MINUTES ADDED TO YOUR RUN TIME
■, Up, ⊙, ✕

Entering the following codes will toggle the cheat on and off:

BIG TIRES
Down, ⊙, ⊙, Down

SLOW
■, ▲, ⊙, ✕

LOW GRAVITY
Up, Up, Up, Up

SPECIAL BAR ALWAYS FULL
Left, Down, ▲, ⊙, Up, Left, ▲, ■

GRIND BALANCE BAR
Left, ⊙, ■, ▲, ■, ⊙, ✕

PERFECT BALANCE
■, Left, Up, Right

ALL SCORES MULTIPLIED BY 10
■, ⊙, ⊙, Up, Down, Down

ALL SCORES DIVIDED BY 10
Down, Down, Up, ●, ●, ●

ALTERNATE COLORS
Down, Down, Down, Down

GRANNY
Up, ●, ✖, ✖, Down, ●

NBA LIVE 2003

Select Roster Management from the Team Management menu. Create a player with the following last names. These characters will be available as free agents.

B-RICH
DOLLABILLS

BUSTA RHYMES
FLIPMODE

DJ CLUE
MIXTAPES

FABOLOUS
GHETTOFAB

HOT KARL
CALIFORNIA

JUST BLAZE
GOODBEATS

NEED FOR SPEED 3: HOT PURSUIT

Enter the following as your name:

ALL CARS AND TRACKS
Enter SPOILT.

MORE CAMERA VIEWS
Enter SEEALL.

EL NINO
Enter ROCKET.

JAGUAR XJR-15
Enter LJAGX.

MERCEDES BENZ CLK-GTR
Enter AMGMRC.

AUTOCROSS TRACK
Enter XCNTRY.

CAVERNS TRACK
Enter XCAV8.

EMPIRE CITY TRACK
Enter MCITYZ.

SCORPIO-7 TRACK
Enter GLDFSH.

SPACE RACE TRACK
Enter MNBEAM.

THE ROOM TRACK
Enter PLAYTM.

NFL GAMEDAY 2003

EASTER EGGS

CODE	EFFECT
BIG PIG	Big Football
LITTLE	Small Players
MUNCHKINS	Small Players
BIGBOYS	Big Players
PANCAKE	Flat Players
ENDURANCE	Better Endurance
EVEN	Even Teams
REDZONE	Redzone Names
ALL BOBO	Players Named Bobo
CREDITS	Credits

RUGRATS STUDIO TOUR

BIG HEAD
Select Tag Race or Diapies of Thunder. Pause the game and press ◉, ▣, ◉, ✕.

SPIDER-MAN 2: ENTER ELECTRO

UNLOCK ALL CHEATS
Select Cheats from the Special Menu and enter **AUNTMAY**.

UNLOCK COSTUMES
Select Cheats from the Special Menu and enter **WASHMCHN**.

UNLOCK GALLERY
Select Cheats from the Special Menu and enter **DRKROOM**.

UNLOCK TRAINING
Select Cheats from the Special Menu and enter **CEREBRA**.

UNLOCK LEVELS
Select Cheats from the Special Menu and enter **NONJYMNT**.

BIG FEET
Select Cheats from the Special Menu and enter **STACEYD**.

BIG HEAD
Select Cheats from the Special Menu and enter **ALIEN**.

DEBUG MODE
Select Cheats from the Special Menu and enter **DRILHERE**.

WHAT IF
Select Cheats from the Special Menu and enter **VVISIONS**.

VV HIGH SCORES
Select Cheats from the Special Menu and enter **VVHISCRS**.

SPYRO: YEAR OF THE DRAGON

Pause your game and enter the following codes to get the desired effect:

2D SPYRO
Left, Right, Left, Right, ⬛, ⬛, ⬛, ⬛, ⬤, ⬤

Enter the code again to change Spyro back to full 3D.

BIG HEAD
Up, ⬛, Up, ⬛, Up, ⬛, ⬤, ⬤, ⬤, ⬤

Enter the code again to change Spyro's head back to normal.

BLACK SPYRO
Up, Left, Down, Right, Up, ⬤, ⬛, ⬛, ⬛, ⬛, Up, Right, Down, Left, Up, Down

BLUE SPYRO
Up, Left, Down, Right, Up, ⬤, ⬛, ⬛, ⬛, ⬛, Up, Right, Down, Left, Up, X

GREEN SPYRO
Up, Left, Down, Right, Up, ⬤, ⬛, ⬛, ⬛, ⬛, Up, Right, Down, Left, Up, ▲

PINK SPYRO
Up, Left, Down, Right, Up, ⬤, ⬛, ⬛, ⬛, ⬛, Up, Right, Down, Left, Up, ⬤

RED SPYRO
Up, Left, Down, Right, Up, ⬤, ⬛, ⬛, ⬛, ⬛, Up, Right, Down, Left, Up, ⬤

YELLOW SPYRO
Up, Left, Down, Right, Up, ⬤, ⬛, ⬛, ⬛, ⬛, Up, Right, Down, Left, Up, Up

ORIGINAL COLOR SPYRO
To change Spyro back to his original color, enter Up, Left, Down, Right, Up, ⬤, ⬛, ⬛, ⬛, ⬛, Up, Right, Down, Left, Up, Left.

CREDITS
Left, Right, Left, Right, Left, Right, ⬛, ⬤, ⬛, ⬤, ⬛, ⬤

CRASH BASH DEMO
Enter this code at the Title Screen. Once there, press ⬛ + ⬛ + ⬛.

STREAK: HOVERBOARD RACING

ALL RIDERS
Select Sierra for Freestyle in a 6 lap Time Trial. Besides Edge as blade 2, turn off other blades and start the race. Pause and quit the race. Then at the rider select, press ⬤ and press Up, Down, ▣, ▣, ▣, ▣, ⬤, SELECT.

STUART LITTLE 2

DEBUG
At the main menu, press Left, ▣, ▣, Right, ▣, ▣, Up, Down.

INVINCIBILITY
At the main menu, press ▣, ⬤, ▣, ⬤, ▣, ⬤, ▣, ⬤.

FULL AMMO
At the main menu, ⬤, ▣, ▣, Up, ⬤, ▣, ▣, Down.

LEVEL SELECT
At the main menu, press ▣, Left, Right, ▣, ▣, Up, Down, ▣.

FLYCAM
At the main menu, press Up, ▣, Down, ▣, ▣, Down, ▣, Up.

ALL MOVIES
At the main menu, press Right, ⬤, ⬤, ⬤, ▣, ▣, Left, ▣.

GALLERY MOVIES
At the main menu, press ⬤, ▣, Left, ▣, ▣, Right, ▣.

INFINITE LIVES
Pause the game, hold ▣, and press ⬤, ⬤, ⬤.

TEST DRIVE 6

Enter the following codes as a name:

EFFECT	CODE
$6,000,000	AKJGQ
All Cars	DFGY
All Tracks	ERERTH
All Quick Race Tracks	CVCVBM
No Quick Race Tracks	OCVCVBM
Shorter Tracks	QTFHYF
All Challenges	OPIOP
No Challenges	OPOIOP
Disable Checkpoint	FFOEMIT
Enable Checkpoint	NOEMIT
Stop the Bomber Mode	RFGTR

TOMB RAIDER CHRONICLES

UNLOCK UNLIMITED HEALTH, AMMO, AND WEAPONS

While in the game, press Select to access your inventory screen. Highlight the Timex and enter the following secret code:

Hold Up + 🔘 + 🔘 + 🔘 + 🔘, and press 🔺.

UNLOCK EVERY ITEM FOR YOUR LEVEL

While in the game, press Select to access your inventory screen. Highlight the Timex and enter the following secret code:

Hold Down + 🔘 + 🔘 + 🔘 + 🔘, and press 🔺.

This also gives you the Special Features option at the main menu.

START AT SECOND ADVENTURE

Highlight the New Game option at the main menu, and enter the following secret code:

Hold 🔘 + Up, then press ❌ to start at the Russian Base.

START AT THIRD ADVENTURE

Highlight the New Game option at the main menu, and enter the following secret code:

Hold 🔘 + Up, then press ❌ to start at the Black Isle.

START AT FOURTH ADVENTURE

Highlight the New Game option at the main menu, and enter the following secret code:

Hold 🔘 + Up, then press ❌ to start at the Tower Block.

TONY HAWK'S PRO SKATER 2

NEVERSOFT CHARACTERS

At the Main Menu, hold 🔘 and press Up, ●, ●, ▲, Right, Up, ●, ▲. This causes the wheel to spin. Create a skater, and give him the name of anyone on the Neversoft team. For example, name your skater Mick West and he'll appear. The best one is Connor Jewett, the son of Neversoft's President. (Don't change the appearance of the kid-sized skaters. It could crash your game.)

You must enter the following codes after pausing the game. While the game is paused, press and hold 🔘, and enter the codes.

JET PACK MODE

Up, Up, Up, Up, ❌, ●, Up, Up, Up, Up, ❌, ●, Up, Up, Up, Up

Hold ▲ to hover.

Press ❌ to turn on the Jetpack.

Press forward to move forward.

FATTER SKATER

❌ (x4), Left, ❌ (x4), Left, ❌ (x4), Left

THINNER SKATER

❌ (x4), ●, ❌ (x4), ●, ❌ (x4), ●

TOGGLE BLOOD ON/OFF
Right, Up, ⬤, ▲

SPECIAL METER ALWAYS YELLOW
❌, ▲, ⬤, ⬤, Up, Left, ▲, ⬤

SUPER SPEED MODE
Down, ⬤, ▲, Right, Up, ⬤, Down, ⬤, ▲, Right, Up, ⬤

UNLOCK EVERYTHING
❌, ❌, ❌, ⬤, ▲, Up, Down, Left, Up, ⬤, ▲, ❌, ▲, ⬤, ❌, ▲, ⬤

BIG HEAD
⬤, ⬤, Up, Left, Left, ⬤, Right, Up, Left

ALL GAPS
Down, Up, Left, Left, ⬤, Left, Up, ▲, ▲, Up, Right, ⬤, ⬤, Up, ❌
This will give you Private Carrera.

ALL SECRET CHARACTERS
⬤, ⬤, Right, ▲, ⬤, Right, ⬤, ▲, Right, ⬤, Right, Up, Up, Left, Up, ⬤

MOON PHYSICS
❌, ⬤, Left, Up, Down, Up, ⬤, ▲

DOUBLE MOON PHYSICS
Left, Up, Left, Up, Down, Up, ⬤, ▲, Left, Up, Left, Up, Down, Up, ⬤, ▲

$5000
❌, Down, Left, Right, Down, Left, Right

100,000 POINTS IN COMPETITION
⬤, ⬤, Right, ⬤, ⬤, Right, ⬤, ⬤, Right
This will end the competition.

ACCESS ALL LEVELS
Up, ▲, Right, Up, ⬤, ▲, Right, Up, Left, ⬤, ⬤, Up, ⬤, ⬤, Up, Right

STATS AT 5
Up, ⬤, ▲, Up, Down

STATS AT 6
Down, ●, ▲, Up, Down

STATS AT 7
Left, ●, ▲, Up, Down

STATS AT 8
Right, ●, ▲, Up, Down

STATS AT 9
●, ●, ▲, Up, Down

STATS AT 13
✕, ▲, ●, ✕, ✕, ✕, ●, ▲, Up, Down

STATS AT ALL 10S
✕, ▲, ●, ●, ▲, Up, Down

SKIP TO RESTART
●, ▲, Right, Up, Down, Up, Left, ●, ▲, Right, Up, Down, Up, Left, ●, Up, Left, ▲

CLEAR GAME WITH CURRENT SKATER
●, Left, Up, Right, ●, Left, Up, Right, ✕, ●, Left, Up, Right, ●, Left, Up, Right

KID MODE
●, Up, Up, Left, Left, ●, Up, Down, ●

MIRROR LEVEL
Up, Down, Left, Right, ▲, ✕, ●, ●, Up, Down, Left, Right, ▲, ✕, ●, ●

PERFECT BALANCE
Right, Up, Left, ●, Right, Up, ●, ▲

SLO-NIC MODE
●, Up, ▲, ●, ✕, ▲, ●

WIREFRAME
Down, ●, Right, Up, ●, ▲

SIM MODE
●, Right, Up, Left, ▲, ●, Right, Up, Down

SMOOTH SHADING
Down, Down, Up, ●, ▲, Up, Right

DISCO LIGHTS
Down, Up, ●, ●, Up, Left, Up, ✕

TONY HAWK'S PRO SKATER 3

The menu shakes if the following are entered correctly:

BIG HEAD
Pause the game, hold 🔼 and press Up, ●, Down.

THIN SKATER
Pause the game, hold 🔼 and press ✕ (x4), ●, ✕ (x4), ●, ✕ (x4), ●.

FAT SKATER
Pause the game, hold 🔼 and press ✕ (x4), Left, ✕ (x4), Left, ✕ (x4), Left.

PERFECT BALANCE
Pause the game, hold 🔼 and press Up, Down, Up, Up, ▲, ✕, ▲, ▲.

STUD MODE
Pause the game, hold ⬛ and press ⬤, ▲, Up, Down, Right, Up, ⬤, ▲.

FULL SPECIAL
Pause the game, hold ⬛ and press ▲, Right, Up, ⬤, ▲, Right, Up, ⬤, ▲.

10,000 POINTS
Pause the game, hold ⬛ and press ⬤, ⬤, Right, ⬤, ⬤, Right, ⬤, ⬤, Right.

TURBO
Pause the game, hold ⬛ and press Left, Up, ⬤, ▲.

SLOW MOTION
Pause the game, hold ⬛ and press Left, Left, Up, Left, Left, Up, ✖.

REVERSED LEVEL
Pause the game, hold ⬛ and press Down, Down, ▲, Left, Up, ⬤, ▲

THE WEAKEST LINK

FINAL ROUND PASSWORDS
To get the following players in the Final Round, highlight the indicated character in round 2 and press ⬤ to open the password screen. Enter the password.

PLAYER	HIGHLIGHT	PASSWORD
Allen	Ruth	Right, Right, Left, Left, Up, Up, Left, Right
Amber	Barry	Right, Right, Up, Right, Left, Down, Right, Right
Angela	Steve	Left, Left, Down, Right, Up, Left, Down, Up
Cindy	Eddie	Right, Up, Up, Down, Up, Down, Down, Up
Eddie	Jules	Right, Up, Left, Down, Left, Up, Up, Down
Evelyn	Eddie	Right, Right, Down, Down, Right, Up, Right, Left
Jenny	Frank	Right, Right, Down, Up, Up, Left, Right, Down
Jojo	Ruth	Down, Right, Right, Left, Down, Right, Up, Down
Jules	Karen	Left, Down, Down, Right, Right, Right, Up, Down
Karen	Gary	Down, Down, Right, Up, Up, Down, Down, Up
Mary	Tim	Up, Right, Up, Left, Down, Right, Up, Down
Nick	Ruth	Down, Right, Up, Left, Up, Left, Left, Right
Ravi	Tony	Left, Left, Left, Up, Down, Left, Up, Down
Ruth	Barry	Up, Down, Up, Down, Left, Right, Down, Down
Samantha	Angela	Down, Down, Right, Right, Up, Right, Down, Up
Steve	Tim	Left, Left, Up, Right, Down, Right, Down, Up
William	Jules	Down, Right, Right, Left, Up, Left, Up, Down

WORLD'S SCARIEST POLICE CHASES

ALL BONUSES
At the main menu, press Left, Right, ⬛, ⬛, ⬤, ⬤, ⬛, ⬛.

LEVEL SELECT
At the main menu, press Down, Up, Left, Right, ✖, ▲, ⬤, ⬤.

YU-GI-OH! FORBIDDEN MEMORIES

PASSWORDS

NUMBER	CARD	PASSWORD
001	Blue Eyes White Dragon	89631139
002	Mystical Elf	15025844
003	Hitotsu-Me Giant	76184692
004	Baby Dragon	88819587
005	Ryu-Kishin	15303296
006	Feral Imp	41392891
007	Winged Dragon #1	87796900
008	Mushroom Man	14181608
009	Shadow Specter	40575313
010	Blackland Fire Dragon	87564352
011	Sword Arm of Dragon	13069066
012	Swamp Battleguard	40453765
013	Tyhone	72842870
014	Battle Steer	18246479
015	Flame Swordsman	45231177
016	Time Wizard	71625222
017	Right Leg of the Forbidden One	08124921
018	Left Leg of the Forbidden One	44519536
019	Right Arm of the Forbidden One	70903634
020	Left Arm of the Forbidden One	07902349
021	Exodia the Forbidden	33396948
022	Summoned Skull	70781052
023	The Wicked Worm Beast	06285791
024	Skull Servant	32274490
025	Horn Imp	69669405
026	Battle Ox	05053103
027	Beaver Warrior	32452818
028	Rock Ogre Grotto #1	68846917
029	Mountain Warrior	04931562
030	Zombie Warrior	31339260
031	Koumori Dragon	67724379
032	Two-headed King Rex	94119974
033	Judgeman	30113682
034	Saggi the Dark Clown	66602787
035	Dark Magician	46986414
036	The Snake Hair	29491031
037	Gaia the Dragon Champion	66889139
038	Gaia the Fierce Knight	06368038
039	Curse of Dragon	28279543
040	Dragon Piper	55763552
041	Celtic Guardian	91152256
042	Illusionist Faceless Mage	28546905
043	Karbonala Warrior	54541900

NUMBER	CARD	PASSWORD
044	Rogue Doll	91939608
045	Oscillo Hero #2	27324313
046	Griffore	53829412
047	Torike	80813021
048	Sangan	26202165
049	Big Insect	53606874
050	Basic Insect	89091579
051	Armored Lizard	15480588
052	Hercules Beatle	52584282
053	Killer Needle	88979991
054	Gokibore	15367030
055	Giant Flea	41762634
056	Larvae Moth	87756343
057	Great Moth	14141448
058	Kuriboh	40640057
059	Mammoth Graveyard	40374923
060	Great White	13429800
061	Wolf	49417509
062	Harpie Lady	76812113
063	Harpie Lady Sisters	12206212
064	Tiger Axe	49791927
065	Silver Fang	90357090
066	Kojikocy	01184620
067	Perfectly Ultimate Great Moth	48579379
068	Garoozis	14977074
069	Thousand Dragon	41462083
070	Fiend Kraken	77456781
071	Jellyfish	14851496
072	Cocoon of Evolution	40240595
073	Kairyu-Shin	76634149
074	Giant Soldier of Stone	13039848
075	Man-Eating Plant	49127943
076	Krokodilus	76512652
077	Grappler	02906250
078	Axe Raider	48305365
079	Megazowler	75390004
080	Uraby	01784619
081	Crawling Dragon #2	38289717
082	Red-eyes B. Dragon	74677422
083	Castle of Dark Illusions	00062121
084	Reaper of the Cards	33066139
085	King of Yamimakai	69455834
086	Barox	06840573
087	Dark Chimera	32344688
088	Metal Guardian	68339286
089	Catapult Turtle	95727991

NUMBER	CARD	PASSWORD
090	Gyakutenno Megami	31122090
091	Mystic Horseman	68516705
092	Rabid Horseman	94905343
093	Zanki	30090452
094	Crawling Dragon	67494157
095	Crass Clown	93889755
096	Armored Zombie	20277860
097	Dragon Zombie	66672569
098	Clown Zombie	92667214
099	Pumpking the King of Ghosts	29155212
100	Battle Warrior	55550921
101	Wings of Wicked Flames	92944626
102	Dark Mask	28933734
103	Job Change Mirror	55337339
104	Curtain of the Dark ones	22026707
105	Tomozaurus	46457856
106	Spirit of the Winds	54615781
107	Kagenigen	80600490
108	Graveyard and the Hand of Invitation	27094595
109	Goddess With the Third Eye	53493204
110	Hero of the East	89987208
111	Doma the Angel of Silence	16972957
112	The Witch that Feeds on Life	52367652
113	Dark Gray	09159938
114	White Magical Hat	15150365
115	Kamion Wizard	41544074
116	Nightmare Scorpion	88643173
117	Spirit of the Books	14037717
118	Supporter in the Shadows	41422426
119	Trial of Nightmares	77827521
120	Dream Clown	13215230
121	Sleeping Lion	40200834
122	Yamatano Dragon Scroll	76704943
123	Dark Plant	13193642
124	Ancient Tool	49587396
125	Faith Bird	75582395
126	Orion the Battle King	02971090
127	Ansatsu	48365709
128	Lamoon	75850803
129	Nemuriko	90963488
130	Weather Control	37243151
131	Octoberser	74637266
132	The 13th Grave	00032864
133	Charubin the Fire Knight	37421579
134	Mystical Capture Chain	63515678
135	Fiend's Hand	52800428

NUMBER	CARD	PASSWORD
136	Witty Phantom	36304921
137	Mystery Hand	62793020
138	Dragon Statue	09197735
139	Blue-eyed Silver Zombie	35282433
140	Toad Master	62671448
141	Spiked Snail	98075147
142	Flame Manipulator	34460851
143	Necrolancer the Timelord	61454890
144	Djinn the Watcher of the Wind	97843505
145	The Bewitching Phantom Thief	24348204
146	Temple of Skulls	00732302
147	Monster Egg	36121917
148	The Shadow Who Controls the Dark	63125616
149	Lord of the Lamp	99510761
150	Akihiron	36904469
151	Rhaintumdos of the Red Sword	62403074
152	The Melting Red Shadow	98898173
153	Dokuroize the Grim Reaper	25882881
154	Fire Reaper	53581214
155	Larvas	94675535
156	Hard Armor	20060230
157	Firegrass	53293545
158	Man Eater	93553943
159	Dig Beak	29948642
160	M-Warrior #1	56342351
161	M-Warrior #2	92731455
162	Tainted Wisdom	28725004
163	Lisark	55210709
164	Lord of Zemia	81618817
165	The Judgement Hand	28003512
166	Mysterious Puppeteer	54098121
167	Ancient Jar	81492226
168	Darkfire Dragon	17881964
169	Dark King of the Abyss	53375573
170	Spirit of the Harp	80770678
171	Big Eye	16768387
172	Armaill	53153481
173	Dark Prisoner	89558090
174	Hurricail	15042735
175	Ancient Brain	42431843
176	Fire Eye	88435542
177	Monsturtle	15820147
178	Claw Reacher	41218256
179	Phantom Dewan	77603950
180	Arlownay	14708569
181	Dark Shade	40196604

NUMBER	CARD	PASSWORD
182	Masked Clown	77581312
183	Lucky Trinket	03985011
184	Genin	49370026
185	Eyearmor	64511793
186	Fiend Reflection #2	02863439
187	Gate Deeg	49258578
188	Synchar	75646173
189	Fusionist	01641882
190	Akakieisu	38035986
191	Lala Li-Oon	09430387
192	Key Mace	01929294
193	Turtle Tiger	37313348
194	Terra the Terrible	63308047
195	Doron	36151751
196	Arma Knight	00756652
197	Mech Mole Zombie	63545455
198	Happy Lover	99030164
199	Penguin Knight	36039163
200	Petit Dragon	75356564
201	Frenzied Panda	98818516
202	Air Marmot of Nefariousness	75889523
203	Phantom Ghost	61201220
204	Mabarrel	98795934
205	Dorover	24194033
206	Twin Long Rods #1	60589682
207	Droll Bird	97973387
208	Petit Angel	38142739
209	Winged Cleaver	39175982
210	Hinotama Soul	96851799
211	Kaminarikozou	15510988
212	Meotoko	53832650
213	Aqua Madoor	85639257
214	Kagemusha of the Blue Flame	15401633
215	Flame Ghost	58528964
216	Dryad	84916669
217	B. Skull Dragon	11901678
218	Two-mouth Darkruler	57305373
219	Solitude	84794011
220	Masked Sorcerer	10189126
221	Kumootoko	56283725
222	Midnight Fiend	83678433
223	Roaring Ocean Snake	19066538
224	Trap Master	46461247
225	Fiend Sword	22855882
226	Skull Stalker	54844990
227	Hitodenchak	46718686

NUMBER	CARD	PASSWORD
228	Wood Remains	17733394
229	Hourglass of Life	08783685
230	Rare Fish	80516007
231	Wood Clown	17511156
232	Madjinn Gunn	43905751
233	Dark Titan of Terror	89494469
234	Beautiful Head Huntress	16899564
235	Wodan the Resident of the Forest	42883273
236	Guardian of the Labyrinth	89272878
237	Haniwa	84285623
238	Yashinoki	41061625
239	Vishwar Randi	78556320
240	The Drdek	08944575
241	Dark Assassin	41949033
242	Candle of Fate	47695416
243	Water Element	03732747
244	Dissolverock	40826495
245	Meda Bat	76211194
246	One Who Hunts Souls	03606209
247	Root Water	39004808
248	Master & Expert	75499502
249	Water Omotics	02483611
250	Hyo	38982356
251	Enchanting Mermaid	75376965
252	Nekogal #1	01761063
253	Angelwitch	37160778
254	Embryonic Beast	64154377
255	Prevent Rat	00549481
256	Dimensional Warrior	37043180
257	Stone Armadiller	63432835
258	Beastking of the Swamp	99426834
259	Ancient Sorcerer	36821538
260	Lunar Queen Elzaim	62210247
261	Wicked Mirror	15150371
262	The Little Swordsman of Aile	25109950
263	Rock Ogre Grotto #2	62193699
264	Wing Egg Elf	98582704
265	The Furious Sea King	18710707
266	Princess of Tsurugi	51371017
267	Unknown Warrior of Fiend	97360116
268	Sectarian of Secrets	15507080
269	Versago the Destroyer	50259460
270	Wetha	96643568
271	Megirus Light	23032273
272	Mavelus	59036972
273	Ancient Tree of Enlightenment	86421986

NUMBER	CARD	PASSWORD
274	Green Phantom King	22910685
275	Ground Attacker Bugroth	58314394
276	Ray & Temperature	85309439
277	Gorgon Egg	11793047
278	Petit Moth	58192742
279	King Fog	84686841
280	Protector of the Throne	10071456
281	Mystic Clown	47060154
282	Mystical Sheep #2	83464209
283	Holograph	10859908
284	Tao the Chanter	46247516
285	Serpent Maurauder	82742611
286	Gate Keeper	19737320
287	Ogre of the Black Shadow	45121025
288	Dark Arts	72520073
289	Change Slime	18914778
290	Moon Envoy	45909477
291	Fireyarou	71407486
292	Psychic Kappa	07892180
293	Masaki the Legendary Swordsman	44287299
294	Dragoness the Wiched Knight	70681994
295	Bio Plant	07670542
296	One-eyed Shield Dragon	33064647
297	Cyber Soldier of Dark World	75559356
298	Wicked Dragon with the Ersatz Head	02957055
299	Sonic Maid	38942059
300	Kurama	85705804
301	Legendary Sword	61854111
302	Sword of Dark Destruction	37120512
303	Dark Energy	04614116
304	Axe of Dispair	40619825
305	Laser Cannon Armor	77007920
306	Insect Armor With A Laser Cannon	03492538
307	Elf's Light	39897277
308	Beast Fangs	46009906
309	Steel Shell	02370081
310	Vile Germs	39774685
311	Black Pendant	65169794
312	Silver Bow and Arrow	01557499
313	Horn of Light	38552107
314	Horn of the Unicorn	64047146
315	Dragon Treasure	01435851
316	Electro-Whip	37820550
317	Cyber Shield	63224564
318	Elegant Egotist	90219263
319	Mystical Moon	36607978

NUMBER	CARD	PASSWORD
320	Stop Defense	63102017
321	Malevolent Nuzzeler	99597615
322	Violet Crystal	15052462
323	Book of Secret Arts	91595718
324	Invigoration	98374133
325	Machine Conversion Factory	25769732
326	Raise Body Heat	51267887
327	Follow Wind	98252586
328	Power of Kaishin	77027445
329	Dragon Capture Jar	50045299
330	Forest	87430998
331	Wasteland	23424603
332	Mountain	50913601
333	Sogen	86318356
334	Umi	22702055
335	Yami	59197169
336	Dark Hole	53129443
337	Raigeki	12580477
338	Mooyan Curry	58074572
339	Red Medicine	38199696
340	Goblin's Secret Remedy	11868825
341	Soul of the Pure	47852924
342	Dian Keto the Cure Master	84257639
343	Sparks	76103675
344	Hinotama	46130346
345	Final Flame	73134081
346	Ookazi	19523799
347	Tremendose Fire	46918794
348	Swords of Revealing Light	72302403
349	Spellbinding Circle	18807108
350	Dark Piercing Light	45895206
351	Yaranzo	71280811
352	Kanan the Swordmistress	12829151
353	Takriminos	44073668
354	Stuffed Animal	71068263
355	Megasonic Eye	07562372
356	Super War-Lion	33951077
357	Yamadron	70345785
358	Seiyaryu	06740720
359	Three-legged Zombie	33734439
360	Zera the Mant	69123138
361	Flying Penguin	05628232
362	Millennium Shield	32012841
363	Fairy's Gift	68401546
364	Black Luster Soldier	05405694
365	Fiend's Mirror	31890399

NUMBER	CARD	PASSWORD
366	Labyrinth Wall	67284908
367	Jirai Gumo	94773007
368	Shadow Ghoul	30778711
369	Wall Shadow	63182310
370	Labyrinth Tank	99551425
371	Sanga of the Thunder	25955164
372	Kazejin	62340868
373	Suijin	98434877
374	Gate Guardian	25833572
375	Dungeon Worm	51228280
376	Monster Tamer	97612389
377	Ryu-Kishin Powered	24611934
378	Swordstalker	50005633
379	La Jinn the Mystical Genie	97590747
380	Blue Eyes Ultimate Dragon	23995346
381	Toon Alligator	59383041
382	Rude Kaiser	26378150
383	Parrot Dragon	62762898
384	Dark Rabbit	99261403
385	Bickuribox	25655502
386	Harpie's Pet Dragon	52040216
387	Mystic Lamp	98049915
388	Pendulum Machine	24433920
389	Giltia the D. Knight	51828629
390	Launcher Spider	87322377
391	Zoa	24311372
392	Metalzoa	50705071
393	Zone Eater	86100785
394	Steel Scorpion	13599884
395	Dancing Elf	59983499
396	Ocubeam	86088138
397	Leghul	12472242
398	Ooguchi	58861941
399	Swordsman from the Foreign Land	85255550
400	Emperor of the Land and Sea	11250655
401	Ushi oni	48649353
402	Monster Eye	84133008
403	Leogun	10538007
404	Tatsunootoshigo	47922711
405	Saber Slasher	73911410
406	Yaiba Robo	10315429
407	Machine King	46700124
408	Giant Mech-Soldier	72299832
409	Metal Dragon	09293977
410	Mechanical Spider	45688586
411	Bat	72076281

NUMBER	CARD	PASSWORD
412	Giga-Tech Wolf	08471389
413	Cyber Soldier	44865098
414	Shovel Crusher	71950093
415	Mechanicalchacer	07359741
416	Blocker	34743446
417	Blast Juggler	70138455
418	Golgoil	07526150
419	Giganto	33621868
420	Cyber-Stein	69015963
421	Cyber Commander	06400512
422	Jinzo #7	32809211
423	Dice Armadillo	69893315
424	Sky Dragon	95288024
425	Thunder Dragon	31786629
426	Stone D.	68171737
427	Kaiser Dragon	94566432
428	Magician of Faith	31560081
429	Goddess of Whim	67959180
430	Water Magician	93343894
431	Ice Water	20848593
432	Waterdragon Fairy	66836598
433	Ancient Elf	93221206
434	Beautiful Beast Trainer	29616941
435	Water Girl	55014050
436	White Dolphin	92409659
437	Deepsea Shark	28593363
438	Metal Fish	55998462
439	Bottom Dweller	81386177
440	7 Colored Fish	23771716
441	Mech Bass	50176820
442	Aqua Dragon	86164529
443	Sea King Dragon	23659124
444	Turu-Purun	59053232
445	Guardian of the Sea	85448931
446	Aqua Snake	12436646
447	Giant Red Snake	58831685
448	Spike Seadra	85326399
449	30,000-Year White Turtle	11714098
450	Kappa Avenger	48109103
451	Kanikabuto	84103702
452	Zarigun	10598400
453	Millennium Golem	47986555
454	Destroyer Golem	73481154
455	Barrel Rock	10476868
456	Minomushi Warrior	46864967
457	Stone Ghost	72269672

NUMBER	CARD	PASSWORD
458	Kaminari Attack	09653271
459	Tripwire Beast	45042329
460	Bolt Escargot	12146024
461	Bolt Penguin	48531733
462	The Immortal of Thunder	84926738
463	Electric Snake	11324436
464	Wing Eagle	47319141
465	Punished Eagle	74703140
466	Skull Red Bird	10202894
467	Crimson Sunbird	46696593
468	Queen Bird	73081602
469	Armed Ninja	09076207
470	Magical Ghost	46474915
471	Soul Hunter	72869010
472	Air Eater	08353769
473	Vermillion Sparrow	35752363
474	Sea Kamen	71746462
475	Sinister Serpent	08131171
476	Ganigumo	34536276
477	Aliensection	70924884
478	Insect Soldiers of the Sky	07019529
479	Cockroach Knight	33413638
480	Kuwagata Alpha	60802233
481	Burglar	06297941
482	Pragtical	33691040
483	Garvas	69780745
484	Amoeba	95174353
485	Korogashi	32569498
486	Boo Koo	68963107
487	Flower Wolf	95952802
488	Rainbow Flower	21347810
489	Barrel Lily	67841515
490	Needle Ball	94230224
491	Peacock	20624263
492	Hoshinigen	67629977
493	Maha Vailo	93013676
494	Rainbow Marine Mermaid	29402771
495	Musicain King	56907389
496	Wilmee	92391084
497	Yado Karu	29380133
498	Morinphen	55784832
499	Kattapillar	81179446
500	Dragon Seeker	28563545
501	Man-Eater Bug	54652250
502	D. Human	81057959
503	Turtle Raccoon	17441953

NUMBER	CARD	PASSWORD
504	Fungi of the Musk	53830602
505	Prisman	80234301
506	Gale Dogra	16229315
507	Crazy Fish	53713014
508	Cyber Saurus	89112729
509	Bracchio-Raidus	16507828
510	Laughing Flower	42591472
511	Bean Soldier	84990171
512	Cannon Soldier	11384280
513	Guardian of the Throne Room	47879985
514	Brave Scizzar	74277583
515	The Statue of Easter Island	10262698
516	Muka Muka	46657337
517	Sand Stone	73051941
518	Boulder Tortoise	09540040
519	Fire Kraken	46534755
520	Turtle Bird	72929454
521	Skullbird	08327462
522	Monstrous Bird	35712107
523	The Bistro Butcher	71107816
524	Star Boy	08201910
525	Spirit of the Mountain	34690519
526	Neck Hunter	70084224
527	Milus Radiant	07489323
528	Togex	33878931
529	Flame Cerberus	60862676
530	Eldeen	06367785
531	Mystical Sand	32751480
532	Gemini Elf	69140098
533	Kwagar Hercules	95144193
534	Minar	32539892
535	Kamakiriman	68928540
536	Mechaleon	94412545
537	Mega Thunderball	21817254
538	Niwatori	07805359
539	Corroding Shark	34290067
540	Skelengel	60694662
541	Hanehane	07089711
542	Misairuzame	33178416
543	Tongyo	69572024
544	Dharma Cannon	96967123
545	Skelgon	32355828
546	Wow Warrior	69750536
547	Griggle	95744531
548	Bone Mouse	21239280
549	Frog the Jam	68638985

NUMBER	CARD	PASSWORD
550	Behegon	94022093
551	Dark Elf	21417692
552	Winged Dragon #2	57405307
553	Mushroom Man #2	93900406
554	Lava Battleguard	20394040
555	Tyhone #2	56789759
556	The Wandering Doomed	93788854
557	Steel Ogre Grotto #1	29172562
558	Pot the Trick	55567161
559	Oscillo Hero	82065276
560	Invader from Another Planet	28450915
561	Lesser Dragon	55444629
562	Needle Worm	81843628
563	Wretched Ghost of the Attic	17238333
564	Great Mammoth of Goldfine	54622031
565	Man-Eating Black Shark	80727036
566	Yormungarde	17115745
567	Darkworld Thorns	43500484
568	Anthrosaurus	89904598
569	Drooling Lizard	16353197
570	Trakadon	42348802
571	B. Dragon Jungle King	89832901
572	Empress Judge	15237615
573	Little D.	42625254
574	Witch of the Black Forest	78010363
575	Ancient One of the Deep Forest	14015067
576	Giant Scorpion of the Tundra	41403766
577	Crow Goblin	77998771
578	Leo Wizard	04392470
579	Abyss Flower	40387124
580	Patrol Robo	76775123
581	Takuhee	03170832
582	Dark Witch	35565537
583	Weather Report	72053645
584	Binding Chain	08058240
585	Mechanical Snail	34442949
586	Greenkappa	61831093
587	Mon Larvas	07225792
588	Living Vase	34320307
589	Tentacle Plant	60715406
590	Beaked Snake	06103114
591	Morphing Jar	33508719
592	Muse-A	69992868
593	Giant Turtle Who Feeds on Flames	96981563
594	Rose Spectre of Dunn	32485271
595	Fiend Reflection #1	68870276

NUMBER	CARD	PASSWORD
596	Ghoul With An Appetite	95265975
597	Pale Beast	21263083
598	Little Chimera	68658728
599	Violent Rain	94042337
600	Key Mace #2	20541432
601	Tenderness	57935140
602	Penguin Soldier	93920745
603	Fairy Dragon	20315854
604	Obese Marmot of Nefariousness	56713552
605	Liquid Beast	93108297
606	Twin Long Rods #2	29692206
607	Great Bill	55691901
608	Shining Friendship	82085619
609	Bladefly	28470714
610	Electric Lizard	55875323
611	Hiro's Shadow Scout	81863068
612	Lady of Faith	17358176
613	Twin-headed Thunder Dragon	54752875
614	Hunter Spider	80141480
615	Armored Starfish	17535588
616	Hourglass of Courage	43530283
617	Marine Beast	29929832
618	Warrior of Tradition	56413937
619	Rock Spirit	82818645
620	Snakeyashi	29802344
621	Succubus Knight	55291359
622	Ill Witch	81686058
623	The Thing that Hides in the Mud	18180762
624	High Tide Gyojin	54579801
625	Fairy of the Fountain	81563416
626	Amazon of the Seas	17968114
627	Nekogal #2	43352213
628	Witch's Apprentice	80741828
629	Armored Rat	16246527
630	Ancient Lizard Warrior	43230671
631	Maiden of the Moonlight	79629370
632	Stone Ogre Grotto	15023985
633	Winged Egg of New Life	42418084
634	Night Lizard	78402798
635	Queen's Double	05901497
636	Blue Winged Crown	41396436
637	Trent	78780140
638	Queen of the Autumn Leaves	04179849
639	Amphibious Bugroth	40173854
640	Acid Crawler	77568553
641	Invader of the Throne	03056267

NUMBER	CARD	PASSWORD
642	Mystical Sheep #1	30451366
643	Disk Magician	76446915
644	Flame Viper	02830619
645	Royal Guard	39239728
646	Gruesome Goo	65623423
647	Hyosube	02118022
648	Machine Attacker	38116136
649	Hibikime	64501875
650	Whiptail Crow	91996584
651	Kunai with Chain	37390589
652	Magical Labyrinth	64389297
653	Warrior Elimination	90873992
654	Salamandra	32268901
655	Cursebraker	69666645
656	Eternal Rest	95051344
657	Megamorph	22046459
658	Metalmorph	68540058
659	Winged Trumpeter	94939166
660	Stain Storm	21323861
661	Crush Card	57728570
662	Eradicading Aerosol	94716515
663	Breath of Light	20101223
664	Eternal Drought	56606928
665	Curse of the Millennium Shield	83094937
666	Yamadron Ritual	29089635
667	Gate Guardian Ritual	56483330
668	Bright Castle	82878489
669	Shadow Spell	29267084
670	Black Luster Ritual	55761792
671	Zera Ritual	81756897
672	Harpie's Feather Duster	18144506
673	War-Lion Ritual	54539105
674	Beastry Mirror Ritual	81933259
675	Ultimate Dragon	17928958
676	Commencement Dance	43417563
677	Hamburger Recipe	80811661
678	Revival of Sengenjin	16206366
679	Novox's Prayer	43694075
680	Curse of Tri-Horned Dragon	79699070
681	House of Adhesive Tape	15083728
682	Eatgaboon	42578427
683	Bear Trap	78977532
684	Invisible Wire	15361130
685	Acid Trap Hole	41356845
686	Widespread Ruin	77754944
687	Goblin Fan	04149689

NUMBER	CARD	PASSWORD
688	Bad Reaction to Simochi	40633297
689	Reverse Trap	77622396
690	Fake Trap	03027001
691	Revival of Serpent Night Dragon	39411600
692	Turtle Oath	76806714
693	Contruct of Mask	02304453
694	Resurrection of Chakra	39399168
695	Puppet Ritual	05783166
696	Javelin Beetle Pact	41182875
697	Garma Sword Oath	78577570
698	Cosmo Queen's Prayer	04561679
699	Revival of Skeleton Rider	31066283
700	Fortress Whale's Oath	77454922
701	Performance of Sword	04849037
702	Hungery Burger	30243636
703	Sengenjin	76232340
704	Skull Guardian	03627449
705	Tri-Horned Dragon	39111158
706	Serpent Night Dragon	66516792
707	Skull Knight	02504891
708	Cosmo Queen	38999506
709	Charka	65393205
710	Crab Turtle	91782219
711	Mikazukinoyaiba	38277918
712	Meteor Dragon	64271667
713	Meteor B. Dragon	90660762
714	Firewing Pegasus	27054370
715	Psyco Puppet	63459075
716	Garma Sword	90844184
717	Javelin Beetle	26932788
718	Fortress Whale	62337487
719	Dokurorider	99721536
720	Mask of Shine and Dark	25110231
721	Dark	76792184
722	Magician of Black Chaos	30208479

PLAYSTATION® 2

The Games

AGASSI TENNIS GENERATION

ALL PLAYERS
At the Main Menu, press 🔳, 🔳, 🔵, ◉, ⊗, ◉.

AIRFORCE DELTA STRIKE

SELF DESTRUCT
Pause the game and press Up, Up, Down, Down, Left, Right, Left, Right, ⊗, ◉.

REFILL HP AND MISSILES
Pause the game and press Up, Up, Down, Down, Left, Right, Left, Right, L3, R3.

ALIAS

LEVEL SELECT
Complete the game, then press 🔳 + 🔳 at the new game screen.

ALIEN HOMINID

HATS FOR 2-PLAYER GAME
Go to the Options and rename your alien one of the following:

abe

april

behemoth

cletus

dandy

goodman

grrl

princess

superfly

ALTER ECHO

RESTORE HEALTH
Press Up, Up, Down, Down, Left, Right, Left, Right, then ⊕ + Right during gameplay.

RESTORE TIME DILATION
Press Up, Up, Down, Down, Left, Right, Left, Right, then ⊕ + Up during gameplay.

APE ESCAPE: PUMPED & PRIMED

ALL GADGETS
Complete Story Mode. At the mode select, hold 🔘 + 🔘 + 🔘 + 🔘 to access the password screen. Enter Go Wild!.

DISABLE ALL GADGETS CHEAT
Complete Story Mode. At the mode select, hold 🔘 + 🔘 + 🔘 + 🔘 to access the password screen. Enter Limited!.

NORMAL DIFFICULTY
Complete Story Mode. At the mode select, hold 🔘 + 🔘 + 🔘 + 🔘 to access the password screen. Enter NORMAL!.

HARD DIFFICULTY
Complete Story Mode. At the mode select, hold 🔘 + 🔘 + 🔘 + 🔘 to access the password screen. Enter HARD!.

ATV OFFROAD FURY 3

UNLOCK EVERYTHING…OTHER THAN THE FURY BIKE
Select Player Profile from the options. Then, select Enter Cheat and enter **!SLACKER!**. This will not give the Fury.

ALL ATV'S IN TRAINING
Select Player Profile from the options. Then, select Enter Cheat and enter NOSKILLS.

ALL RIDER GEAR
Select Player Profile from the options. Then, select Enter Cheat and enter FITS.

$1500
Select Player Profile from the options. Then, select Enter Cheat and enter +foodstamps+.

MUSIC VIDEOS
Select Player Profile from the options. Then, select Enter Cheat and enter ROCKNROLL.

THE BARD'S TALE

During a game, hold ⊞ + ⊞ and enter the following:

EVERYTHING ON (SILVER AND ADDERSTONES)
Up, Up, Down, Down, Left, Right, Left, Right

FULL HEALTH AND MANA
Left, Left, Right, Right, Up, Down, Up, Down

CAN'T BE HURT
Right, Left, Right, Left, Up, Down, Up, Down

CAN'T BE STRUCK
Left, Right, Left, Right, Up, Down, Up, Down

DAMAGE X100
Up, Down, Up, Down, Left, Right, Left, Right

UNLOCK LEVELS
Right, Right, Left, Left, Up, Down, Up, Down

DEBUG MENU
During a game, hold ⊞ and press Right.

BATTLESTAR GALACTICA

MINI-SERIES MATERIALS
Select Extras and enter the following:
Left, Up, Left, Left, Down, Left, Up, Down.
Up, Up, Down, Down, Right, Up, Right, Down.
Right, Right, Down, Down, Left, Left, Up, Up.
Down(x4), Left(x4).
Up (x3), Down (x3), Left, Right.
Up, Left, Up, Right, Up, Left, Up, Right.
Right(x4), Down, Down, Left, Left.
Right, Right, Up, Up, Left, Left, Up, Up.

STARBUCK AND APOLLO AS WINGMEN
Select Extras and press Down, Down, Left, Down, Down, Up, Right, Right.

BUTT UGLY MARTIANS: ZOOM OR DOOM

ALL RACERS
During a game, hold ⊞ + ⊞ and press ⬢, ⬛, ✖, ⬤.

CABELA'S DEER HUNT 2005 SEASON

GPS
At the equipment menu, press ⚠, ⬛, ⬤, L1, R2, ❌.

CASTLE SHIKIGAMI 2

EXTRA CREDITS
Earn an extra credit for each hour of gameplay.

YOUNG FUMIKO
At the character select, highlight Fumiko and press Right, Right.

CATWOMAN

UNLOCK HIDDEN SURPRISES THROUGHOUT THE COMIC
Enter 1940 as a Vault code.

CHAMPIONS OF NORRATH: REALMS OF EVERQUEST

LEVEL 20 CHARACTER
During a game, press and hold L1 + R2 + ⚠ + ⬤. This makes your character level 20 with 75,000 coins and 999 skill points. This does *not* increase your character's main attributes.

DOG'S LIFE

CHEAT MENU
During a game, press ● (Bark), ● (Bark), ● (Bark), hold ● (Growl), hold ● (Growl), hold ● (Growl), Left, Right, Down (Fart).

DROME RACERS

INSTANT WIN
At the main menu, press Left, Right, Left, Right, Up, Down, Up, Down, ●, ▲, ●. Press L3 during a race to win.

ALL TRACKS
At the main menu, press Left, Right, Left, Right, Up, Down, Up, Down, ▲, ▲, ✕.

PURPLE RAIN
At the main menu, press Left, Right, Left, Right, Up, Down, Up, Down, Up, Down, ● (x3).

WIREFRAME MODE
At the main menu, press Left, Right, Left, Right, Up, Down, Up, Down, ●, ●, ✕.

DUEL MASTERS

ALL LOCATIONS
At the map screen, hold R3 and press ● (x3).

4 OF EVERY CARD AND UNLOCK CHUCK IN ARCADE MODE
At the deck building screen, hold R3 and press ⬛, ⬛, ⬛.

PLAYER 1 LOSES SHIELD
During a duel, hold R3 and press ▲, ●, ✕. Release R3.

PLAYER 2 LOSES SHIELD
During a duel, hold R3 and press ▲, ●, ✕. Release R3.

PLAYER 1 GAINS SHIELD
During a duel, hold R3 and press ✕, ●, ▲. Release R3.

PLAYER 2 GAINS SHIELD
During a duel, hold R3 and press ✕, ●, ▲. Release R3.

PLAYER 1 WINS
During a duel, hold R3 and press ⬛, ⬛, ⬛.

PLAYER 2 WINS
During a duel, hold R3 and press ⬛, ⬛, ⬛.

TURN OFF DECK OUTS
During a duel, hold R3 and press ● (x3).

ESPN NBA 2K5

ALL 24/7 ITEMS
Create a player named RAY GRAHAM.

ESPN NFL 2K5

Enter these codes as your case sensitive VIP name:

ALL CRIB ITEMS
Enter CribMax.

ALL MILESTONE
Enter MadSkilz.

1,000,000 CRIB POINTS
Enter PhatBank.

FIFA STREET

ALL APPAREL
At the main menu, hold ⬜ + ⬤ and press Right, Right, Left, Up (x3), Down, Left.

MINI PLAYERS
Pause the game, hold ⬜ + ⬤ and press Up, Left, Down, Down, Right, Down, Up, Left.

NORMAL SIZE PLAYERS
Pause the game, hold ⬜ + ⬤ and press Right, Right, Up, Down, Down, Left, Right, Left.

FISHERMAN'S BASS CLUB

UNBREAKABLE LINE
On the first cast, press ⬜, ⬜, ⬜, ⬜, ⬤, ⬤, ⬜.

FISHERMAN'S CHALLENGE

AI DIFFICULTY INCREASE BY 10%
At the main tournament screen, press Up, Up, Down, Down, Left, Right, Left, Right, ⬜, ⬜.

FREE FISH AT NIGHT
At the Free Fish Time setting, press Up, Up, Down, Down, Left, Right, Left, Right, ⬜, ⬜.

HIDE THE FISH MOOD LENS
While in casting mode, press Up, Up, Down, Down, Left, Right, Left, Right, ⬜, ⬜.

RETRIEVE LINE WITHOUT WINDING ANALOG STICK
While retrieving a fishing line, Up, Up, Down, Down, Left, Right, Left, Right, ⬜, ⬜.

TURN OFF UNDERWATER VIEW
While using trolling motor, Up, Up, Down, Down, Left, Right, Left, Right, ⬜, ⬜.

FUTURE TACTICS: THE UPRISING

LEVEL SKIP
At the game select screen, press ⬜, ⬤, ⬜, ⬜, ⬜, ⬤, ⬜, ⬜, ⬜.

UNLIMITED TURNS AND MOVEMENT
During a game, press Up, Up, Down, Down, Left, Right, Left, Left, ⬜, ⬜.

BIG HEADS
During a game, press Up, Left, Down, Left, Down, Up, Up, Left.

DISCO MODE
During a game, press ⬜, Left, ⬜, Left, ⬜, Right, ⬜, Right.

LOW GRAVITY
During a game, press Up (x6), Down, Right, Up.

GHOST MASTER

LEVEL SKIP
At the level select, hold ⬜ + ⬜ and press ⬤ (x4). Hold ⬜ to skip levels.

MAXIMUM PLASMA
During a game, hold ⬜ + ⬜ and press ⬤, ⬤, ⬤, ⬤.

GOBLIN COMMANDER: UNLEASH THE HORDE

During a game, press and hold ⬛ + ⬛ + ▲ + Down until a message appears in the upper-right corner of the screen. After doing so, you can enter the following codes. Re-enter the code to disable it.

GOD MODE
Press ⬛ (x3), ⬛ (x3), ⬛, ⬛, ▲, ⬛.

AUTOMATIC WIN
Press ⬛, ⬛, ⬛ (x3), ⬛, ⬛, ▲ (x3).

ALL LEVEL ACCESS
Press ▲ (x3), ⬛, ▲ (x3).

Start a Campaign to select a level.

FOG OF WAR
Press ⬛, ⬛, ⬛, ⬛, ⬛, ⬛, ▲, ▲, ⬛, ⬛.

GAME SPEED X1/2
Press ⬛ (x5), ▲ (x4), ⬛.

GAME SPEED X2
Press ⬛ (x5), ⬛, ▲, ⬛ (x3).

GOLD +100
Press ⬛, ⬛ (x4), ⬛, ▲, ⬛ (x3).

SOULS +100
Press ⬛, ⬛ (x4), ⬛, ▲, ⬛ (x3).

GODZILLA: SAVE THE EARTH

CHEAT MENU
At the main menu, press and hold ⬛, ●, ⬛ in order, then let go of ●, ⬛, ⬛ in order. Now you can enter the following cheats.

ALL CITIES
Enter 659996.

ALL MONSTERS
Enter 525955.

UNLOCK CHALLENGES
Enter 975013.

HEALTH REGENERATES
Enter 536117.

ENERGY DOES NOT REGENERATE
Enter 122574.

INDESTRUCTIBLE BUILDINGS
Enter 812304.

100,000 POINTS
Enter 532459.

150,000 POINTS
Enter 667596.

200,000 POINTS
Enter 750330.

PLAYER 1: 4X DAMAGE
Enter 259565.

PLAYER 1: INFINITE ENERGY
Enter 819342.

PLAYER 1: INVISIBLE
Enter 531470.

PLAYER 1: INVULNERABLE
Enter 338592.

PLAYER 2: 4X DAMAGE
Enter 927281.

PLAYER 2: INFINITE ENERGY
Enter 324511.

PLAYER 2: INVISIBLE
Enter 118699.

PLAYER 2: INVULNERABLE
Enter 259333.

PLAYER 3: 4X DAMAGE
Enter 500494.

PLAYER 3: INFINITE ENERGY
Enter 651417.

PLAYER 3: INVISIBLE
Enter 507215.

PLAYER 3: INVULNERABLE
Enter 953598.

PLAYER 4: 4X DAMAGE
Enter 988551.

PLAYER 4: INFINITE ENERGY
Enter 456719.

PLAYER 4: INVISIBLE
Enter 198690.

PLAYER 4: INVULNERABLE
Enter 485542.

GALLERY
Enter 294206.

GODZILLA FINAL WARS
Enter 409014.

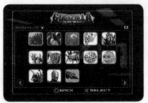

GRADIUS V

You can use one of these each level completed.

DOUBLE SHOT POWER
After the first boss, pause the game and press Up, Up, Down, Down, Left, Right, Left, Right, ▦, ▦.

LASER POWER
After the first boss, pause the game and press Up, Up, Down, Down, Left, Right, Left, Right, ▦, ▦.

GRAN TURISMO 4

EXTRA TRACKS FOR ARCADE MODE
Play through the indicated amount of days to unlock the corresponding track in Arcade Mode.

DAYS	UNLOCK
15	Deep Forest Raceway
29	Opera Paris
43	Fuji Speedway 80s
57	Special Stage Route 5
71	Suzuka Circuit
85	Twin Ring Motegi Road Course East Short
99	Grand Valley Speedway
113	Hong Kong
127	Suzuka Circuit West Course
141	Fuji Speedway 2005 GT
155	Ice Arena
169	Apricot Hill Raceway
183	Cote d Azur
197	Tahiti Maze
211	Twin Ring Motegi Road Course
225	George V Paris
239	Cathedral Rocks Trail I
253	Costa di Amalfi
267	Circuit de la Sarthe 1
281	Autumn Ring
309	Chamonix
309	Infineon Raceway Stock Car Course
323	Fuji Speedway 2005 F
337	Tsukuba Circuit Wet
351	Circuit de la Sarthe 2 (Not chicaned)

GRETZKY NHL 2005

EVERYTHING
At the Unlockables screen, press Start to bring up the code entry. Enter shoenloc.

GROWLANSER GENERATIONS

ALL ARMOR, GEMS AND MAX MONEY
At the world map, press Up, Right, ⬛, ⬛, Down, ⬛, ⬛ Up, Down, ⬛, ⬛, Right, Left, ⬤, ⬤, ⬤.

HOT SHOTS GOLF FORE!

Select Password from the Options menu and enter the following codes to enable these cheats:

ALL CHARACTERS AVAILABLE IN VS MODE
Enter REZTWS.

ALOHA BEACH RESORT COURSE IN SHOP
Enter XSREHD.

BAGPIPE CLASSIC COURSE IN SHOP
Enter CRCNHZ.

PRICE REDUCTION SALE IN SHOP
Enter MKJEFQ.

BLUE LAGOON C.C. COURSE IN SHOP
Enter WVRJQS.

MINI-GOLF 2 G.C. IN SHOP
Enter RVMIRU.

DAY DREAM G.C. IN SHOP
Enter OQUTNA.

SILKROAD CLASSIC COURSE IN SHOP
Enter ZKOGJM.

UNITED FOREST G.C. IN SHOP
Enter UIWHLZ.

WESTERN VALLEY COUNTRY CLUB COURSE AVAILABLE IN SHOP
Enter LIBTFL .

WILD GREEN C.C. COURSE IN SHOP
Enter YZLOXE.

CAPSULE 01 IN SHOP
Enter WXAFSJ.

CAPSULE 2 IN SHOP
Enter OEINLK.

CAPSULE 3 IN SHOP
Enter WFKVTG.

CAPSULE 4 IN SHOP
Enter FCAVDO.

CAPSULE 5 IN SHOP
Enter YYPOKK.

CAPSULE 6 IN SHOP
Enter GDQDOF.

CAPSULE 7 IN SHOP
Enter HHXKPV.

CAPSULE 8 IN SHOP
Enter UOKXPS.

CAPSULE 9 IN SHOP
Enter LMIRYD.

CAPSULE 10 IN SHOP
Enter MJLJEQ.

CAPSULE 11 IN SHOP
Enter MHNCQI

LOWER TOURNEY STAGE
Enter XKWGFZ.

CADDIE CLANK AVAILABLE IN SHOP
Enter XCQGWJ.

CADDIE DAXTER AVAILABLE IN SHOP
Enter WSIKIN.

CADDIE KAYLA AVAILABLE IN SHOP
Enter MZIMEL.

CADDIE KAZ AVAILABLE IN SHOP
Enter LNNZJV.

CADDIE MOCHI AVAILABLE IN SHOP
Enter MYPWPA .

CADDIE SIMON AVAILABLE IN SHOP
Enter WRHZNB.

CADDIE SOPHIE AVAILABLE IN SHOP
Enter UTWIVQ.

BEGINNER'S BALL AVAILABLE IN SHOP
Enter YFQJJI.

BIR AIR BALL AVAILABLE IN SHOP
Enter CRCGKR.

INFINITY BALL AVAILABLE IN SHOP
Enter DJXBRG.

PIN HOLE BALL AVAILABLE IN SHOP
Enter VZLSGP.

SIDESPIN BALL AVAILABLE IN SHOP
Enter JAYQRK.

TURBO SPIN BALL AVAILABLE IN SHOP
Enter XNETOK.

100T HAMMER CLUB (B-CLASS) AVAILABLE IN SHOP
Enter NFSNHR.

UPGRADE 100T HAMMER CLUB (A-CLASS) AVAILABLE IN SHOP
Enter BVLHSI.

UPGRADE 100T HAMMER CLUB (S-CLASS) AVAILABLE IN SHOP
Enter MCSRUK.

BIG AIR CLUB (B-CLASS) AVAILABLE IN SHOP
Enter DLJMFZ.

UPGRADE BIG AIR CLUB (A-CLASS) AVAILABLE IN SHOP
Enter TOSXUJ.

UPGRADE BIG AIR CLUB (S-CLASS) AVAILABLE IN SHOP
Enter JIDTQI.

INFINITY CLUB AVAILABLE IN SHOP
Enter RZTQGV.

UPGRADE INFINITY CLUB (A-CLASS) AVAILABLE IN SHOP
Enter WTGFOR.

UPGRADE INFINITY CLUB (S-CLASS) AVAILABLE IN SHOP
Enter EIPCUL.

PIN HOLE CLUB (B-CLASS) AVAILABLE IN SHOP
Enter DGHFRP .

UPGRADE PIN HOLE CLUB (A-CLASS) AVAILABLE IN SHOP
Enter TTIMHT.

UPGRADE PIN HOLE CLUB (S-CLASS) AVAILABLE IN SHOP
Enter RBXVEL.

UPGRADE TURBO SPIN CLUB (A-CLASS) AVAILABLE IN SHOP
Enter NIWKWP.

UPGRADE TURBO SPIN CLUB (S-CLASS) AVAILABLE IN SHOP
Enter DTIZAB.

EXTRA POSE CAM AVAILABLE IN SHOP
Enter UEROOK.

EXTRA SWING CAM AVAILABLE IN SHOP
Enter RJIFQS.

EXTRA VIDEO AVAILABLE IN SHOP
Enter DPYHIU.

HECKLETS AVAILABLE IN SHOP
Enter DIXWFE.

HSG CD/VOICE AVAILABLE IN SHOP
Enter UITUGF.

HSG CD/MUSIC AVAILABLE IN SHOP
Enter PAJXLI .

HSG RULES AVAILABLE IN SHOP
Enter FKDHDS.

LANDING GRID AVAILABLE IN SHOP
Enter MQTIMV.

REPLAY CAM A AVAILABLE IN SHOP
Enter PVJEMF.

REPLAY CAM B AVAILABLE IN SHOP
Enter EKENCR.

REPLAY CAM C AVAILABLE IN SHOP
Enter ZUHHAC.

MENU CHARACTER BRAD AVAILABLE IN SHOP
Enter ZKJSIO.

MENU CHARACTER PHOEBE AVAILABLE IN SHOP
Enter LWVLCB.

MENU CHARACTER RENEE AVAILABLE IN SHOP
Enter AVIQXS.

WALLPAPER SET 2 AVAILABLE IN SHOP
Enter RODDHQ.

MIKE'S COSTUME AVAILABLE IN SHOP
Enter YKCFEZ.

LIN'S COSTUME AVAILABLE IN SHOP
Enter BBLSKQ.

MEL'S COSTUME AVAILABLE IN SHOP
Enter ARFLCR.

PHOEBE'S COSTUME AVAILABLE IN SHOP
Enter GJBCHY.

HOT WHEELS: VELOCITY X

ALL CARS AND TRACKS
At the main menu, hold ⬜ + ⬜ and press ◉, ⬛, ⬛, ▲, ✖

KARAOKE REVOLUTION

Enter the following codes at the Title screen or before you enter Character Select screen. Saving is disabled with these cheats.

ANIMATION GENDER SWAP
Press ▣, ▣, ▣, ▣, Down, Down, Up, Up, Down, ▣.

BANANA MICROPHONE
Press ▣, ▣, ▣, ▣, Down, Down, Right, Left, ◉, Up.

BIG EYES
Press Up, Up, Down, Down, Left, Right, Left, Right, ◉, ▣.

BIG HEAD
Press Up, Down, Up, Down, Right, Right, Left, Left, ◉, ▣.

GLASS CHARACTER
Press Right, Left, Right, Left, Up, Up, Down, Down, ◉, ▣.

OILSLICK CHARACTER
Press Left, Right, Left, Right, Down, Down, Up, Up, ◉, ▣.

SMALL HEAD
Press Down, Down, Up, Up, Left, Right, Down, Up, ◉, ▣.

T2 CHARACTER
Press ▣, ▣, Right, ▣, Up, Up, Left, Up, ▣, ◉.

TOOTHBRUSH MICROPHONE
Press ▣, ▣, ▣, ▣, Down, Down, ◉, ▣, ◉, ▣.

TOUGH CROWD AUDIO
Press ▣ (x4), Up, Left, Right, Down, ◉, ◉.

UNLOCK ALL CHARACTERS
Press ▣, ▣, ▣, ▣, Up, Left, Up, Right, ▣, ▣.

UNLOCK ALL OUTFITS
Press ▣, ◉, ◉, ▣, Up, Down, Left, Right, ▣, ▣.

UNLOCK ALL SONGS
Press ◉, ▣, ◉, ▣, Up, Down, Left, Right, ▣, ▣.

UNLOCK ALL VENUES
Press ◉, ◉, ◉, ◉, Up, Down, Left, Down, ▣, ▣.

UNLOCK ALL VIDEOS
Press ▣, ▣, ◉, ◉, Up, Left, Right, Up, ▣, ▣.

WRAITH CHARACTER
Press ▣, ▣, ▣, ▣, ▣, ◉, Right, Right, ▣, ▣.

KARAOKE REVOLUTION VOLUME 2

Cheats

At the Title screen, enter the following:

ALL SONGS
Press ●, ▲, Down, Left, Up, Right, L2, R2, Start.

ALL CHARACTERS
Press Up, ●, Right, ●, ●, Left, ●, Up, L1, R1.

ALL COSTUMES
Press Up, ●, Left, ●, ●, Down, ●, Right, L1, R1.

ALL VENUES
Press ●, ▲, Right, Up, Left, Down, L2, R2, Start.

GAME INFORMER T-SHIRT FOR ANGELA
Press Down, R1(2), L1(2), ●, Right, ●, L1, R1.

GAMEPRO T-SHIRT
Press Down, R1, Up, R1, R1, Down, R1, Up, Down, ●.

GAME STAR T-SHIRT
Press Up, R1, Right, R1(2), Left, R1, Down, ●, ●.

HARMONIX T-SHIRT FOR ISHANI
Press L1, ●, Up, ●, ●, L1, Down, Down, R1.

KONAMI T-SHIRT FOR DWAYNE
Press Right, R1, Right, R1, ●, Right, ●, ●, Down, Left.

PSM T-SHIRT FOR DEVRON
Press Left, Right, Left, L1, R1, Down, Up, Up, ●, ●.

More Cheats

Select Cheat Collection from Extras and enter the following or enter during a game:

BANANA MICROPHONE
Press L1, L1, R3, R2, Right, Down, ●, Left, Up, ●.

DWAYNE DOLL MICROPHONE
Press ●, R3, ●, L1, R1, L2, ●, Up, ●, ●.

TOOTHBRUSH MICROPHONE
Press L1, L1, R3, R2, Right, Left, Down, Up, ●, ●.

BIG HEAD CHARACTER
Press Down (x3), Up, L1, L2, R2, L1, ●, ●.

SMALL HEAD CHARACTER
Press Right, Right, Up, Up, L2, R2, R2, L1, L1.

BIG EYE CHARACTER
Press ●(x4), ●, Down, Down, R2, L2, L1.

GLASS CHARACTER
Press ●, ●, ●, R2, L2, L2, Down, Right, Right, Up.

OIL SLICK CHARACTER
Press R2, L2, L2, R2, ●, Down, ●, Up, Left, Right.

MERCURY CHARACTER
Press ●, L1, R2, Up, Up, Left, Left, ●, ●, L1.

WRAITH CHARACTER
Press R2, Left, L1, Right, Up, Up, ●, ●, Down, L2.

Even More Cheats

Select Cheat Collection from Extras and enter the following:

TOUGH CROWD
Press Right, Up, ● (x3), R2, L1, L1, L2, Down.

PIRATE CROWD
Press ●, ●, Left, Left, L2, L1, R2, L1, ●, L2.

ROBOT CROWD
Press ●, ●, Right, Right, R2, L1, L1, R2, ●, R2.

ZOMBIE CROWD
Press Left, L1, R2, ●, ●, L2, L2, L1, Left, Left.

KARAOKE REVOLUTION VOLUME 3

BANANA MICROPHONE
Score gold at each venue in Showtime mode. At the Extras menu, press Down, Up, Left, Right, ●, ●, ●, ● at Cheat Collection 1.

BIG EYED CHARACTER
Score gold at each venue in Showtime mode. At the Extras menu, press ●, ●, ●, ●, Down, Left, Left, Down at Cheat Collection 1.

DWAYNE DOLL MICROPHONE
Score gold at each venue in Showtime mode. At the Extras menu, press ●, ●, R3, ●, Up, Down, Right, Left at Cheat Collection 1.

TOOTHBRUSH MICROPHONE
Score gold at each venue in Showtime mode. At the Extras menu, press L2, R2, ●, ●, Down, Up, Left, L3 at Cheat Collection 1.

BIG HEAD CHARACTER
Score gold at each venue in Showtime mode. At the Extras menu, press ●, ●, ●, ●, Up, Right, Down, Left at Cheat Collection 2.

FISH MICROPHONE
Score gold at each venue in Showtime mode. At the Extras menu, press ●, Down, Up, Left, ●, ●, L2, R1 at Cheat Collection 2.

MERCURY CHARACTER
Score gold at each venue in Showtime mode. At the Extras menu, press Down, Down, Right, Left, Right, Left, ●, ● at Cheat Collection 2.

WRAITH CHARACTER
Score gold at each venue in Showtime mode. At the Extras menu, press L2, R2, Right, Right, ●, ●, L1, R1 at Cheat Collection 2.

GLASS CHARACTER
Score gold at each venue in Showtime mode. At the Extras menu, press Down, R2, L1, L2, R1, ●, ●, ● at Cheat Collection 3.

ICE CREAM MICROPHONE
Score gold at each venue in Showtime mode. At the Extras menu, press ●, ●, ●, ●, R2, L2, R1, L1 at Cheat Collection 3.

OIL SLICK CHARACTER
Score gold at each venue in Showtime mode. At the Extras menu, press L3, L3, R2, R1, L2, R1, Down, Up at Cheat Collection 3.

SMALL HEAD CHARACTER
Score gold at each venue in Showtime mode. At the Extras menu, press ●, R2, L2, R1, L1, Down, Down, Up at Cheat Collection 3.

ALIEN CROWD
Score gold at each venue in Showtime mode. At the Extras menu, press Up, Up, Down, ●, ●, R2, L2, ● at Cheat Collection 4.

PIRATE CROWD
Score gold at each venue in Showtime mode. At the Extras menu, press Down, L2, R2, R2, R1, ●, ●, ● at Cheat Collection 4.

ROBOT CROWD
Score gold at each venue in Showtime mode. At the Extras menu, press L3, Down, Down, R1, ●, ●, ●, ● at Cheat Collection 4.

TOUGH AUDIO CROWD
Score gold at each venue in Showtime mode. At the Extras menu, press ●, R1, R2, L1, L2, Right, Right, Down at Cheat Collection 4.

ZOMBIE CROWD
Score gold at each venue in Showtime mode. At the Extras menu, press ●, ●, ●, ●, Up, Right, Right, Up at Cheat Collection 4.

KATAMARI DAMACY

COMETS

Finish a "Make a Star" level under a certain time to earn a comet. Use the following table to find the times you must beat to earn a comet.

LEVEL	FINISH WITHIN...
Make a Star 1	1 minute
Make a Star 2	3 minutes
Make a Star 3	4 minutes
Make a Star 4	6 minutes
Make a Star 5	8 minutes
Make a Star 6	8 minutes
Make a Star 7	8 minutes
Make a Star 8	12 minutes
Make a Star 9	15 minutes
Make the Moon	20 minutes

KYA: DARK LINEAGE

BONUS GALLERY
At the main menu, press ●, Up, ●, Right, Down, Down, ●, Left.

RESTORE LIFE
Pause the game and press ▣, ▣, ▣, ▣, Up, Up, Left, ●, Right, ●, Start.

SHRINK JAMGUT
Pause the game and press ▣, ▣, ●, ▣, ▣, ▣, Left, ▣, ▲.

LEGO STAR WARS: THE VIDEO GAME

Extras

Pause the game and select Extras to toggle these cheats on and off.

INVINCIBILITY
At Dexter's Diner, select Enter Code and enter 4P●●8U.

BIG BLASTERS
At Dexter's Diner, select Enter Code and enter IG72X4.

CLASSIC BLASTERS
At Dexter's Diner, select Enter Code and enter L449HD.

SILLY BLASTERS
At Dexter's Diner, select Enter Code and enter NR37W1.

BRUSHES
At Dexter's Diner, select Enter Code and enter SHRUB1.

TEA CUPS
At Dexter's Diner, select Enter Code and enter PUCEAT.

MINIKIT DETECTOR
At Dexter's Diner, select Enter Code and enter LD116B.

MOUSTACHES
At Dexter's Diner, select Enter Code and enter RP924W.

PURPLE
At Depxter's Diner, select Enter Code and enter YD77GC.

SILHOUETTES
At Dexter's Diner, select Enter Code and enter MS999Q.

Characters

These codes make each character available for purchase from Dexter's Diner.

BATTLE DROID
At Dexter's Diner, select Enter Code and enter 987UYR.

BATTLE DROID (COMMANDER)
At Dexter's Diner, select Enter Code and enter EN11K5.

BATTLE DROID (GEONOSIS)
At Dexter's Diner, select Enter Code and enter LK42U6.

BATTLE DROID (SECURITY)
At Dexter's Diner, select Enter Code and enter KF999A.

BOBA FETT
At Dexter's Diner, select Enter Code and enter LA811Y.

CLONE
At Dexter's Diner, select Enter Code and enter F8B4L6.

CLONE (EPISODE III)
At Dexter's Diner, select Enter Code and enter ER33JN.

CLONE (EPISODE III, PILOT)
At Dexter's Diner, select Enter Code and enter BHU72T.

CLONE (EPISODE III, SWAMP)
At Dexter's Diner, select Enter Code and enter N3T6P8.

CLONE (EPISODE III, WALKER)
At Dexter's Diner, select Enter Code and enter RS6E25.

COUNT DOOKU
At Dexter's Diner, select Enter Code and enter 14PGMN.

DARTH MAUL
At Dexter's Diner, select Enter Code and enter H35TUX.

DARTH SIDIOUS
At Dexter's Diner, select Enter Code and enter A32CAM.

DISGUISED CLONE
At Dexter's Diner, select Enter Code and enter VR832U.

DROIDEKA
At Dexter's Diner, select Enter Code and enter DH382U.

GENERAL GRIEVOUS
At Dexter's Diner, select Enter Code and enter SF321Y.

GEONOSIAN
At Dexter's Diner, select Enter Code and enter 19D7NB.

GRIEVOUS' BODYGUARD
At Dexter's Diner, select Enter Code and enter ZTY392.

GONK DROID
At Dexter's Diner, select Enter Code and enter U63B2A.

JANGO FETT
At Dexter's Diner, select Enter Code and enter PL47NH.

KI-ADI MUNDI
At Dexter's Diner, select Enter Code and enter DP55MV.

KIT FISTO
At Dexter's Diner, select Enter Code and enter CBR954.

LUMINARA
At Dexter's Diner, select Enter Code and enter A725X4.

MACE WINDU (EPISODE III)
At Dexter's Diner, select Enter Code and enter MS952L.

PADMÉ
At Dexter's Diner, select Enter Code and enter 92UJ7D.

PK DROID
At Dexter's Diner, select Enter Code and enter R840JU.

PRINCESS LEIA
At Dexter's Diner, select Enter Code and enter BEQ82H.

REBEL TROOPER
At Dexter's Diner, select Enter Code and enter L54YUK.

ROYAL GUARD
At Dexter's Diner, select Enter Code and enter PP43JX.

SHAAK TI
At Dexter's Diner, select Enter Code and enter EUW862.

SUPER BATTLE DROID
At Dexter's Diner, select Enter Code and enter XZNG01.

4-HIT COMBO, FRODO

MADDEN NFL 2005

CHEAT CARDS

Select Madden Cards from the My Madden menu. Then, select Madden Codes and enter the following:

CHEAT	CODE
3rd Down, Opponent only get 3 downs to get a 1st	Z28X8K
5th Down, Get 5 downs to get a 1st Down	P66C4L
Aloha Stadium	G67F5X
Bingo!, Defensive interceptions increase by 75% for game	J33I8F
Da Bomb, Unlimited pass range	B61A8M
Da Boot, Unlimited field goal range	I76X3T
Extra Credit, Awards points for interceptions and sacks	M89S8G
First and Fifteen, your opponent must get 15 yards to get a 1st down	V65J8P
First and Five, 1st down yards are set to 5	O72E9B
Fumbilitis, Opponents fumbles increase by 75% for game	R14B8Z
Human Plow, Break tackle increases by 75% for game	L96J7P
Lame Duck, Opponent will throw lob passes	D57R5S
Mistake Free, Can't fumble or throw interceptions	X78P9Z
Mr. Mobility, Your QB can't get sacked	Y59R8R
Super Bowl XL	O85P6I
Super Bowl XLI	P48Z4D
Super Bowl XLII	T67R1O
Super Bowl XXXIX	D58F1B
Super Dive, Diving distance increases by 75%	D59K3Y
Tight Fit, Opponents uprights will be narrow	V34L6D
Unforced Errors, Opponent fumble ball when he jukes	L48G1E

CLASSIC TEAM CARDS

Select Madden Cards from the My Madden menu. Then, select Madden Codes and enter the following:

TEAM	CODE
1958 Colts	P74X8J
1966 Packers	G49P7W
1968 Jets	C24W2A
1970 Browns	G12N1I

TEAM	CODE
1972 Dolphins	R79W6W
1974 Steelers	R12D9B
1976 Raiders	P96Q8M
1977 Broncos	O18T2A
1978 Dolphins	G97U5X
1980 Raiders	K71K4E
1981 Chargers	Y27N9A
1982 Redskins	F56D6V

TEAM	CODE
1984 Dolphins	X23Z8H
1985 Bears	F92M8M
1986 Giants	K44F2Y
1988 49ers	F77R8H
1990 Eagles	G95F2Q
1991 Lions	I89F4I
1992 Cowboys	I44A1O
1993 Bills	Y66K3O

CHEERLEADER/PUMP UP THE CROWD CARDS

Select Madden Cards from the My Madden menu. Then, select Madden Codes and enter the following:

TEAM	CODE
Patriots	O59P9C
49ers	X61T6L
Bengals	Y22S6G
Bills	F26S6X
Broncos	B85U5C
Browns	B65Q1L
Buccaneers	Z55Z7S
Cardinals	Q91W5L
Chargers	Q68S3F
Chiefs	T46M6T
Colts	M22Z6H
Cowboys	J84E3F
Dolphins	E88T2J
Eagles	Q88P3Q
Falcons	W86F3F
Giants	L13Z9J

TEAM	CODE
Jaguars	K32C2A
Jets	S45W1M
Lions	C18F4G
Packers	K26Y4V
Panthers	M66N4D
Raiders	G92O9E
Rams	W73B8X
Ravens	P98T6C
Redskins	N19D6Q
Saints	R99G2F
Seahawks	A35T8R
Steelers	C98I2V
Texans	R74G3W
Titans	Q81V4N
Vikings	E26H4L

GOLD PLAYER CARDS

Select Madden Cards from the My Madden menu. Then, select Madden Codes and enter the following:

PLAYER	CODE
Aaron Brooks	J95K1J
Aaron Glenn	Q48E9G
Adewale Ogunleye	C12E9E
Ahman Green	T86L4C
Al Wilson	G72G2R
Alan Faneca	U32S9C
Amani Toomer	Z75G6M
Andre Carter	V76E2Q
Andre Johnson	E34S1M
Andy Reid	N44K1L
Anquan Boldin	S32F7K
Antonio Winfield	A12V7Z
Bill Cowher	S54T6U

PLAYER	CODE
Brad Hopkins	P44A8B
Bret Farve	L61D7B
Brian Billick	L27C4K
Brian Dawkins	Y47B8Y
Brian Simmons	S22M6A
Brian Urlacher	Z34J4U
Brian Westbrook	V46I2I
Bubba Franks	U77F2W
Butch Davis	G77L6F
Byron Leftwich	C55V5C
Carson Palmer	O36V2H
Casey Hampton	Z11P9T
Chad Johnson	R85S2A

PLAYER	CODE	PLAYER	CODE
Chad Pennington	B64L2F	Jason Taylor	O33S6I
Champ Bailey	K89O9E	Jason Webster	M74B3E
Charles Woodson	F95N9J	Jeff Fisher	N62B6J
Chris Hovan	F14C6J	Jeff Garcia	H32H7B
Clinton Portis	Z28D2V	Jeremy Newberry	J77Y8C
Corey Simon	R11D7K	Jeremy Shockey	R34X5T
Courtney Brown	R42R75	Jerry Porter	F71Q9Z
Curtis Martin	K47X3G	Jerry Rice	K34F8S
Dallas Coach	O24U1Q	Jevon Kearse	A78B1C
Damien Woody	E57K9Y	Jim Haslett	G78R3W
Damien Woody	F78I1I	Jim Mora Jr.	N46C3M
Dante Hall	B23P8D	Jimmy Smith	I22J5W
Dat Nguyen	Q8612S	Joe Horn	P91A1Q
Daunte Culpepper	O6209K	John Fox	Q98R7Y
Dave Wannstedt	W73D7D	Jon Gruden	H61I8A
David Boston	A25I9F	Josh Mccown	O33Y4X
David Carr	C16E2Q	Julian Peterson	M89J8A
Dennis Erickson	J83E3T	Julius Peppers	X54O4Z
Dennis Green	C18J7T	Junior Seau	W26K6Q
Derrick Brooks	P93I9Q	Kabeer Gbaja-Biamala	U16I9Y
Derrick Mason	S98P3T	Keith Brooking	E12P4S
Deuce Mcallister	D11H4J	Keith Bulluck	M63N6V
Dexter Coakley	L35K1A	Kendrell Bell	T96C7J
Dexter Jackson	G16B2I	Kevan Barlow	A23T5E
Dick Vermeil	F68V1W	Kevin Mawee	L76E6S
Dom Capers	B97I6R	Kris Jenkins	W63O3K
Domanick Davis	L58S3J	Kyle Boller	A72F9X
Donie Edwards	E18Y5Z	Kyle Turley	Y46A8V
Donovin Darius	Q11T7T	Ladainian Tomlinson	M64D4E
Donovon Mcnabb	T98J1I	Lavar Arrington	F19Q8W
Donte Stallworth	R75W3M	Laveranues Coles	R98I5S
Drew Bledsoe	W73M3E	Lawyer Milloy	M37Y5B
Dre'Bly	Z68W8J	La'roi Glover	K24L9K
Dwight Freeney	G76U2L	Lee Suggs	Z94X6Q
Edgerrin James	A75D7X	Leonard Davis	H14M2V
Ed Reed	G18Q2B	Lovie Smith	L38V3A
Eric Moulds	H34Z8K	Marc Bulger	U66B4S
Flozell Adams	R54T1O	Marcel Shipp	R42X2L
Fred Taylor	I87X9Y	Marcus Stroud	E56I5O
Grant Wistrom	E46M4Y	Marcus Trufant	R46T5U
Herman Edwards	O19T2T	Mark Brunell	B66D9J
Hines Ward	M12B8F	Marshell Faulk	U76G1U
Jack Del Rio	J22P9I	Marty Booker	P51U4B
Jake Delhomme	M86N9F	Marty Booker	H19Q2O
Jake Plummer	N74P8X	Marty Shottenheimer	D96A7S
Jamie Sharper	W27I7G	Marvin Harrison	T11E8O

PLAYER	CODE	PLAYER	CODE
Marvin Lewis	P24S4H	Roy Williams	J76C6F
Matt Hasselback	R68D5F	Rudi Johnson	W26J6H
Michael Bennett	W81W2J	Sam Madison	Z87T5C
Michael Strahan	O66T6K	Samari Rolle	C69H4Z
Michael Vick	H67B1F	Santana Moss	H79E5B
Mike Alstott	D89F6W	Seattle Coach	V58U4Y
Mike Brown	F12J8N	Shaun Alexander	C95Z4P
Mike Martz	R64A8E	Shaun Ellis	Z54F2B
Mike Mularkey	C56D6E	Shaun Rogers	J97X8M
Mike Rucker	K8906S	Shawn Springs	J95K1J
Mike Shanahan	H15L5Y	Simeon Rice	S62F9T
Mike Sherman	F84X6K	Stephen Davis	E39X9L
Mike Tice	Y31T6Y	Steve Mariucci	V74Q3N
New England Coach	N24L4Z	Steve Mcnair	S36T1I
Nick Bernett	X95I7S	Steve Smith	W91O2O
Norv Turner	F24K1M	T.J. Duckett	P67E1I
Olin Kreutz	R17R20	Takeo Spikes	B83A6C
Orlando Pace	U42U9U	Tedy Bruschi	K28Q3P
Patrick Surtain	H58T9X	Terence Newman	W57Y5P
Peerless Price	X75V6K	Terrell Suggs	V71A9Q
Peter Warrick	D86P80	Tiki Barber	T43A2V
Peyton Manning	L48H4U	Todd Heap	H19M1G
Plaxico Burress	K18P6J	Tom Brady	X22V7E
Priest Holmes	X91N1L	Tom Coughlin	S71D6H
Quentin Jammer	V55S3Q	Tony Dungy	Y96R8V
Randy Moss	W79U7X	Tony Gonzalez	N46E9N
Ray Lewis	B94X6V	Torry Holt	W96U7E
Reggie Wayne	R29S8C	Travis Henry	F36M2Q
Rex Grossman	C46P2A	Trent Green	Y46M4S
Rich Gannon	Q69I1Y	Ty Law	F13W1Z
Richard Seymore	L69T4T	Walter Jones	G57P1P
Ricky Williams	P19V1N	Washington Coach	W63V9L
Rod Smith	V22C4L	Will Shields	B52S8A
Rodney Harrison	O84I3J	Zach Thomas	U63I3H
Rondel Barber	J72X8W		

MEGA MAN X8

PLAY AS ALIA
At the title screen, press Down, ▥, Up, ▥, ●, ✕, ▲, ●.

PLAY AS LAYER
At the title screen, press ●, ●, Right, ✕, ▥.

BATTLE CUTMAN
At the title screen, press Left, ●, Up, ▲, Down, ✕, Right, ●, ▥, ▥, ▥, ▥.

SIGMA BLADE
At the title screen, press L3, L3, R3, L3, L3, L3, L3, L3, R3, L3, L3, R3.

BLACK ZERO
At the title screen, press ▥, ▥, ▥, ▥, ▥, ▥, ▥, ▥.

PALLETE
At the title screen, press ▥, ✕, Left, ●, ●.

ULTIMATE ARMOR X
At the title screen, press Left, Left, Left, Right, Right, Right, Left, Left, Left, Left, Right, Right, Right, Right.

WHITE AXL
At the title screen, press 🔲, 🔲, 🔲, 🔲, 🔲, 🔲, 🔲, 🔲, 🔲, 🔲.

MIDNIGHT CLUB 3: DUB EDITION

ALL CITIES AND RACES IN ARCADE MODE
Select Cheat Codes from the Options and enter urbansprawl, roadtrip or crosscountry.

NO DAMAGE
Select Cheat Codes from the Options and enter ontheroad.

ARGO SPECIAL MOVE
Select Cheat Codes from the Options and enter dfens.

ROAR SPECIAL MOVE
Select Cheat Codes from the Options and enter Rjnr.

ZONE SPECIAL MOVE
Select Cheat Codes from the Options and enter allin.

ADD $1 TO CAREER MONEY
Select Cheat Codes from the Options and enter kubmir.

SUBTRACT $1 OF CAREER MONEY
Select Cheat Codes from the Options and enter rimbuk.

BUNNY HEAD
Select Cheat Codes from the Options and enter getheadl.

CHROME HEAD
Select Cheat Codes from the Options and enter haveyouseenthisboy.

FLAMING HEAD
Select Cheat Codes from the Options and enter trythisathome.

SNOWMAN HEAD
Select Cheat Codes from the Options and enter getheadm.

PUMPKIN HEAD
Select Cheat Codes from the Options and enter getheadk.

YELLOW SMILE HEAD
Select Cheat Codes from the Options and enter getheadj.

MLB 2005

ALL PLAYERS
At the Main menu, press Left, Up, Left, Right, Down, Right, Left, Up.

ALL TEAMS
At the Main menu, press Left, Right, Right, Down, Down, Left, Up, Up.

ALL UNIFORMS
At the Main menu, press Up, Down, Right, Left, Down, Right, Down, Up.

ALL STADIUMS
At the Main menu, press Down, Up, Left, Right, Up, Right, Up, Down.

BEANS
At the Main menu, press Right(6), Left, Down.

BIG BALL
At the Main menu, press Up, Up, Right, Left, Up, Up, Right, Left.

BIG HEAD
At the Main menu, press Left, Right, Left, Right, Up, Down, Up, Down.

SMALL HEAD
At the Main menu, press Up, Down, Up, Up, Right (x3), Left.

BLACK AND WHITE
At the Main menu, press Up, Up, Down, Down, Left, Right, Left, Right.

FASTER RUNNERS
At the Main menu, press Left, Right, Left, Right, Left, Right, Up, Up.

SLOWER RUNNERS
At the Main menu, press Right, Left, Right, Left, Right, Left, Down, Down.

SUPER PITCH BREAK
At the Main menu, press Right, Left, Right, Left, Right, Left, Up, Up.

SUPER PITCH SPEED
At the Main menu, press Up (x3), Left (x3), Left, Right.

SUPER SIX PITCHES
At the Main menu, press Down, Up, Down, Right (x4), Left.

MLB SLUGFEST: LOADED

CHEATS

At the Match-Up screen, press ●, ▲, and ● to enter the following codes, then press the appropriate direction. For example, for 16" Softball press ●(x2), ▲(x4), ●(x2), then press Down.

CODE	ENTER	CODE	ENTER
Bone Bat	0-0-1 Up	Dolphin Team	1-0-2 Down
Blade Bat	0-0-2 Up	Dwarf Team	1-0-3 Down
Ice Bat	0-0-3 Up	Eagle Team	2-1-2 Right
Log Bat	0-0-4 Up	Evil Clown Team	2-1-1 Down
Spike Bat	0-0-5 Up	Gladiator Team	1-1-3 Down
Whiffle Bat	0-0-4 Right	Horse Team	2-1-1 Right
Max Batting	3-0-0 Left	Lion Team	2-2-0 Right
Max Power	0-3-0 Left	Minotaur Team	1-1-0 Down
Max Speed	0-0-3 Left	Napalitano Team	2-3-2 Down
Unlimited Turbo	4-4-4 Down	Olshan Team	2-2-2 Down
Extra Time After Plays	1-2-3 Left	Pinto Team	2-1-0 Right
Little League Mode	1-0-1 Down	Rivera Team	2-2-2 Up
16" Softball	2-4-2 Down	Rodeo Clown Team	1-3-2 Down
Rubber Bball	2-4-2 Up	Scorpion team	1-1-2 Down
Tiny Head	2-0-0 Left	Terry Fitzgerald team	3-3-3 Right
Big Head	2-0-0 Right	Todd McFarlane team	2-2-2 Right
Alien Team	2-3-1 Down	Atlantis stadium	3-2-1 Left
Bobblehead Team	1-3-3 Down	Coliseum stadium	3-3-3 Up
Casey team	2-3-3 Down	Empire Park stadium	3-2-1 Right

CODE	ENTER	CODE	ENTER
Forbidden City stadium	3-3-3 Left	Monument stadium	3-3-3 Down
Midway Park stadium	3-2-1 Down	Rocket Park stadium	3-2-1 Up

MTX: MOTOTRAX

Select Cheats from the Options and enter the following:

FASTER BIKE
Enter jih345.

ALL TRACKS
Enter BA7H.

MAXIMUM AIR
Enter BFB0020.

SKY CAMERA
Enter HIC.

BUTTERFINGER GEAR
Enter B77393.

LEFT FIELD GEAR
Enter 12345.

SOBE GEAR
Enter 50B3.

OFFICER DICK
Enter BADG3.

NOKIA TRICKBOT
Enter HA79000.

SPEED DEMON
Enter 773H999.

SLIPKNOT MAGGOT
Enter 86657457.

SLIPKNOT FMV
Enter 23F7IC5.

ALL FMVS
Enter 23F7ICS.

MVP BASEBALL 2005

ALL STADIUMS, PLAYERS, UNIFORMS AND REWARDS
Create a player named Katie Roy.

RED SOX ST. PATRICK'S DAY UNIFORM
Create a player named Neverlose Sight.

BAD HITTER WITH THIN BAT
Create a player named Erik Kiss.

GOOD HITTER WITH BIG BAT
Create a player named Isaiah Paterson, Jacob Paterson or Keegan Paterson.

BIGGER BODY
Create a player named Kenny Lee.

MX UNLEASHED

Select Cheat Codes from the Options menu, then highlight the desired cheat and press ⬤ to access a keyboard. Enter the following codes.

SUPERCROSS TRACKS
Enter STUPERCROSS.

NATIONAL TRACKS
Enter ECONATION.

FREESTYLE TRACKS
Enter BUSTBIG.

PRO PHYSICS
Enter SWAPPIN.

EXPERT AI
Enter OBTGOFAST.

MACHINES
Enter MINIGAMES.

50CC BIKES
Enter SQUIRRELDOG.

500CC BIKES
Enter BIGDOGS.

CAREER COMPLETION
Enter CLAPPEDOUT.

AI BOWLING
Enter WRECKINGBALL.

MX VS. ATV UNLEASHED

UNLOCK EVERYTHING
Select Cheat Codes from the Options and enter TOOLAZY.

1,000,000 POINTS
Select Cheat Codes from the Options and enter BROKEASAJOKE. After entering the code, press Done multiple times for more points.

ALL PRO RIDERS
Select Cheat Codes from the Options and enter WANNABE.

ALL GEAR
Select Cheat Codes from the Options and enter WARDROBE.

50CC BIKE CLASS
Select Cheat Codes from the Options and enter MINIMOTO.

ALL MACHINES
Select Cheat Codes from the Options and enter LEADFOOT.

ALL FREESTYLE TRACKS
Select Cheat Codes from the Options and enter HUCKIT.

NASCAR 2005: CHASE FOR THE CUP

DALE EARNHARDT
At the Edit Driver screen, enter The Intimidator as your name.

$10,000,000
At the Edit Driver screen, enter Walmart NASCAR as your name.

10,000,000 FANS
At the Edit Driver screen, enter MakeMe Famous as your name.

EXCLUSIVE TRACK
At the Edit Driver screen, enter Walmart Exclusive as your name.

MR. CLEAN PIT CREW
At the Edit Driver screen, enter Clean Crew as your name.

DODGE CARS
At the Edit Driver screen, enter Race Dodge as your name.

DODGE TRACKS
At the Edit Driver screen, enter Dodge Stadium as your name.

LEVI STRAUSS CARS
At the Edit Driver screen, enter Levi Stauss153 as your name.

OLD SPICE CARS
At the Edit Driver screen, enter OldSpice Motorsports as your name.

OLD SPICE TRACKS
At the Edit Driver screen, enter OldSpice Venue as your name.

NBA BALLERS

VERSUS SCREEN CHEATS
You can enter the following codes at the Versus screen. The ● button corresponds to the first number in the code, the ▲ is the second number, and the ● button corresponds to the last number. Press the D-pad in any direction to enter the code.

BIG HEAD CODE

EFFECT	CODE
Big Head	1 3 4
Baby Ballers	4 2 3
Kid Ballers	4 3 3
Young Ballers1	4 4 3
Paper Ballers	3 5 4
Alternate Gear	1 2 3

PAPER BALLERS CODE

ALTERNATE GEAR CODE

PLAY AS COACH CODE

PLAY AS SECRETARY CODE

EFFECT	CODE
Show Shot Percentage	0 1 2
Expanded Move Set	5 1 2
Super Push	3 1 5
Super Block Ability	1 2 4
Great Handles	3 3 2
Unlimited Juice	7 6 3
Super Steals	2 1 5
Perfect Free Throws	3 2 7
Speedy Players	2 1 3
Better Free Throws	3 1 7
Fire Ability	7 2 2
Hotspot Ability	6 2 7
Back-In Ability	1 2 2
2x Juice Replenish	4 3 1
Stunt Ability	3 7 4
Pass 2 Friend Ability	5 3 6

EFFECT	CODE
Alley-Oop Ability	7 2 5
Put Back Ability	3 1 3
Legal Goal Tending	7 5 6
R2R Mode	0 0 8
Play As Coach	5 6 7
Play As Agent	5 5 7
Play As Secretary	5 4 7
Play As BiznezMan-A	5 3 7
Play As BiznezMan-B	5 2 7
Play As Afro Man	5 1 7
Super Back-Ins	2 3 5
Half House	3 6 7
Random Moves	3 0 0
Pygmy	4 2 5
Tournament Mode	0 1 1

PLAY AS AFRO MAN CODE

PHRASE-OLOGY CODES/ALTERNATE GEAR

Select Phrase-ology from the Inside Stuff option and enter the following codes to unlock the Alternate Gear for the corresponding player.

PLAYER	PHRASE
Allan Houston	KNICKER BOCKER PLEASE
Allen Iverson	KILLER CROSSOVER
Alonzo Mourning	ZO
Amare Stoudemire	RISING SUN
Antoine Walker	BALL HAWK
Baron Davis	STYLIN' & PROFILIN'
Ben Wallace	RADIO CONTROLLED CARS
Bill Russell	CELTICS DYNASTY
Bill Walton	TOWERS OF POWER
Carmelo Anthony	NEW TO THE GAME
Chris Webber	24 SECONDS
Clyde Drexler	CLYDE THE GLIDE
Darko Milicic	NBA FASTBREAK
Darryl Dawkins	RIM WRECKER
Dejaun Wagner	NBA HANGTIME
Dikembe Mutumbo	IN THE PAINT
Dominique Wilkins	DUNK FEST
Eddie Jones	BALLER UPRISING
Elton Brand	REBOUND
Emanuel Ginobili	MANU
Gary Payton	GLOVE IS IN LA
George Gervin	THE ICE MAN COMETH
Grant Hill	GONE GOLD WITH IT
Isiah Thomas	TRUE BALLER
Jalen Rose	BRING IT
Jason Kidd	PASS THE ROCK
Jason Terry	BALL ABOVE ALL
Jason Williams	GIVE AND GO

PLAYER	PHRASE
Jerry Stackhouse	STOP DROP AND ROLL
John Stockton	COURT VISION
Julius Irving	ONE ON ONE
Karl Malone	SPECIAL DELIVERY
Kenyon Martin	TO THE HOLE
Kevin Garnett	BOSS HOSS
Kevin McHale	HOLLA BACK
Kobe Bryant	JAPANESE STEAK
Larry Bird	HOOSIER
Latrell Sprewell	SPREE
Lebron James	KING JAMES
Magic Johnson	LAKER LEGENDS
Michael Finley	STUDENT OF THE GAME
Mike Bibby	DREAMS & SCHEMES
Moses Malone	LOST FREESTYLE FILES
Nate "Tiny" Archibald	NATE THE SKATE
Nene Hilario	RAGS TO RICHES
Oscar Robertson	AINT NO THING
Pau Gasol	POW POW POW
Paul Pierce	CELTICS SUPREME
Pete Maravich	PISTOL PETE
Rashard Lewis	FAST FORWARD
Rasheed Wallace	BRING DOWN THE HOUSE
Ray Allen	ALL STAR
Reggie Miller	FROM DOWNTOWN
Richard Hamilton	RIP
Robert Parish	THE CHIEF
Scottie Pippen	PLAYMAKER
Shaquille O'Neal	DIESEL RULES THE PAINT

PLAYER	PHRASE	PLAYER	PHRASE
Shawn Marion	MAKE YOUR MARK	Vince Carter	CHECK MY CRIB
Stephon Marbury	PLATINUM PLAYA	Wally Szczerbiak	WORLD
Steve Francis	ANKLE BREAKER	Walt Frazier	PENETRATE AND PERPETRATE
Steve Francis	RISING STAR		
Steve Nash	HAIR CANADA	Wes Unseld	OLD SCHOOL
Tim Duncan	MAKE IT TAKE IT	Willis Reed	HALL OF FAME
Tony Parker	RUN AND SHOOT	Wilt Chamberlain	WILT THE STILT
Tracy McGrady	LIVING LIKE A BALLER	Yao Ming	CENTER OF ATTENTION

CRIBS

Select Phrase-ology from the Inside Stuff option and enter the following to unlock player cribs.

CRIB	PHRASE
Allen Iverson's Recording Studio	THE ANSWER
Karl Malone's Devonshire Estate	ICE HOUSE
Kobe Bryant's Italian Estate	EURO CRIB
Scottie Pippen's Yacht	NICE YACHT
Yao Ming's Childhood Grade School	PREP SCHOOL

ALLEN IVERSON **KARL MALONE**

KOBE BRYANT **SCOTTIE PIPPEN**

YAO MING

OTHER PHRASE-OLOGY CODES

Select Phrase-ology from the Inside Stuff option and enter the following to unlock that bonus.

BONUS	PHRASE
All Players, Alternate Gear, and Cinemas	NBA BALLERS TRUE PLAYA
Special Movie #1	JUICE HOUSE
Special Movie #2	NBA SHOWTIME
Special Movie #3	NBA BALLERS RULES
Special Movie #4	HATCHET MAN
Special Movie #5	SLAM IT
Special Shoe #2	COLD STREAK
Special Shoe #3	LOST YA SHOES

NBA LIVE 2005

50,000 DYNASTY POINTS
Enter **YISS55CZ0E** as an NBA Live Code.

ALL CLASSICS HARDWOOD JERSEYS
Enter **PRYI234N0B** as an NBA Live Code.

ALL TEAM GEAR
Enter **1NVDR89E⬛** as an NBA Live Code.

ALL SHOES
Enter **FHM389HU80** as an NBA Live Code.

AIR UNLIMITED SHOES
Enter **XVLJD9895V** as an NBA Live Code.

HUARACHE 2K4 SHOES
Enter **VNBA60230T** as an NBA Live Code.

NIKE BG ROLLOUT SHOES
Enter **0984ADF90P** as an NBA Live Code.

NIKE SHOX ELITE SHOES
Enter **2388HDFCBJ** as an NBA Live Code.

ZOOM GENERATION LOW SHOES
Enter **234SDJF9W4** as an NBA Live Code.

ZOOM LEBRON JAMES II SHOES
Enter **1KENZO23XZ** as an NBA Live Code.

ATLANTA HAWKS ALTERNATE UNIFORM
Enter **HDI834NN9N** as an NBA Live Code.

BOSTON CELTICS ALTERNATE UNIFORM
Enter **XCV43MGMDS** as an NBA Live Code.

DALLAS MAVERICKS ALTERNATE UNIFORM
Enter **AAPSEUD09U** as an NBA Live Code.

NEW ORLEANS HORNETS ALTERNATE UNIFORM
Enter **JRE7H4D90F** as a NBA Live Code.

NEW ORLEANS HORNETS ALTERNATE UNIFORM 2
Enter **JRE7H4D9WH** as a NBA Live Code.

SEATTLE SONICS' ALTERNATE UNIFORM
Enter **BHD87YY27Q** as a NBA Live Code.

GOLDEN STATE WARRIORS ALTERNATE UNIFORM
Enter **NAVNY29548** as an NBA Live Code.

NCAA FOOTBALL 2005

PENNANT CODES
At the Pennant Collection, press Select and enter the following:

CODE	EFFECT	CODE	EFFECT
EA Sports	Cuffed Cheat	Great To Be	Florida All-time
Thanks	1st and 15	Great To Be	Florida All-time
Sic Em	Baylor powerup	Uprising	Florida State All-time
For	Blink (ball spotted short)	Hunker Down	Georgia All-time
Registering	Boing (dropped passes)	On Iowa	Iowa All-time
Tiburon	Crossed The Line	Geaux Tigers	LSU All-time
Oskee Wow	Illinois Team Boost	Golden Domer	Notre Dame All-time
Hike	Jumbalaya	Boomer	Oklahoma All-time
Home Field	Molasses Cheat	Go Pokes	Oklahoma State All-time
Elite 11	QB Dud	Lets Go Pitt	Pittsburgh All-time
NCAA	Stiffed	Boiler Up	Purdue All-time
Football	Take Your Time	Orange Crush	Syracuse All-time
Fight	Texas Tech Team Boost	Big Orange	Tennessee All-time
2005	Thread The Needle	Gig Em	Texas A&M All-time
Tech Triumph	Virginia Tech Team Boost	Hook Em	Texas All-time
Blitz	What a Hit	Mighty	UCLA All-time
Fumble	2003 All-Americans	Killer Bucks	Ohio State All-time
Roll Tide	Alabama All-time	Killer Nuts	Ohio State All-time
Raising Cane	Miami All-time	Wahoos	Virginia All-time
Go Blue	Michigan All-time	Ramblinwreck	Georgia Tech Mascot Team
Hail State	Mississippi State All-time	Red And Gold	Iowa St. Mascot Team
Go Big Red	Nebraska All-time	Rock Chalk	Kansas Mascot Team
Rah Rah	North Carolina All-time	On On UK	Kentucky Mascot Team
We Are	Penn State All-time	Go Green	Michigan State Mascot Team
Death Valley	Clemson All-time		
Glory	Colorado All-time	Rah Rah Rah	Minnesota Mascot Team
Victory	Kansas State All-time	Mizzou Rah	Missouri Mascot Team
Quack Attack	Oregon All-time	Go Pack	NC State Mascot Team
Fight On	USC All-time	Go Cats	NU Mascot Team
Bow Down	Washington All-time	Hotty Totty	Ole Miss Mascot Team
Bear Down	Arizona mascot team	Hail WV	West Virginia Mascot Team
WooPigSooie	Arkansas All-time	Go Deacs Go	Wake Forest Mascot Team
War Eagle	Auburn All-time	All Hail	WSU Mascot Team
U Rah Rah	Badgers All-time		

NEED FOR SPEED UNDERGROUND

ALL CIRCUIT TRACKS
At the Main menu, press Down, ☐, ☐, ☐, ☐, ☐, ☐, ☐.

ALL SPRINT TRACKS
At the Main Menu, press Up, ☐, ☐, ☐, ☐, Down, Down, Down.

DRIFT PHYSICS IN ALL MODES
At the Main menu, press ☐, Up, Up, Up, Down, Down, Down, ☐.

LEVEL 1 PERFORMANCE PARTS
At the Main menu, press ☐, ☐, ☐, ☐, Left, Right, Left, Right.

LEVEL 2 PERFORMANCE PARTS
At the main menu, press ☐ (x4), ☐, ☐, Left, Right.

LEVEL 2 VISUAL PARTS
At the Main menu, press Down, Left, Up, Down, ☐, ☐, ☐, ☐.

ACURA INTEGRA
At the Main menu, press ☐, ☐, ☐, ☐, ☐, ☐, Down, Up.

ACURA RSX
At the Main menu, press ☐, ☐, Down, Left, Up, Right, Left, Right.

FORD FOCUS
At the Main menu, press Left, Right, Up, ☐, ☐, ☐, ☐, Up.

HONDA S2000
At the Main menu, press Up, Up, Down, Down, Up, Left, ☐, ☐.

ALL DRAG TRACKS
At the Main Menu, press Right, ☐, Left, ☐, ☐, ☐, ☐, ☐.

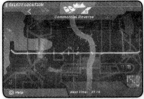

ALL DRIFT TRACKS
At the Main Menu, press Left, Left, Left, Left, Right, ☐, ☐, ☐.

HYUNDAI TIBURON
At the Main menu, press Left, Right, Left, Right, Up, Down, Up, Down.

LOST PROPHETS CAR
At the Main menu, press Up (x3), Right, Down, Down, Up, Right.

MITSUBISHI LANCER
At the Main menu, press Left (x3), ☐, ☐, ☐, ☐, ☐.

MYSTIKAL CAR
At the Main menu, press Up, Right, Up, Up, Down, Right, Up, Right.

NISSAN NISMO
At the Main menu, press Up, Down, Up, Left, Down, Down, Up, Right.

NISSAN 240SX
At the Main menu, press Up, Down, Left, Right, ☐, ☐, ☐, ☐.

NISSAN 350Z
At the Main menu, press Right, Right, Down, Up, ☐, ☐, ☐, ☐.

NISSAN SENTRA
At the Main menu, press Right (x3), ☐, ☐, ☐, ☐, Up.

NISSAN SKYLINE
At the Main menu, press Down, Down, ☐, ☐, ☐, ☐, ☐, Down.

PETEY PABLO CAR
At the Main menu, press Up (x4), Down, Up, Up, Right.

ROB ZOMBIE CAR
At the Main menu, press Up, Left, Up, Up, Down, Left, Up, Right.

SUBARU IMPREZA
At the Main menu, press Up, Down, Down, Up, ▣, Up, ▣, Down.

TOYOTA SUPRA
At the Main menu, press ▣, ▣, ▣, ▣, ▣, ▣, ▣, ▣.

NEED FOR SPEED UNDERGROUND 2

ALL BONUSES
At the title screen, ▣, ▣, ▣, ▣, Up, Down, Right, Left.

ALL CIRCUIT TRACKS
At the title screen, Down, ▣, ▣, ▣, ▣, ▣, ▣, ▣.

$200 IN CAREER MODE
At the title screen, Up, Up, Up, Left, ▣, ▣, ▣, Down.

HUMMER H2 CAPONE
At the title screen, Up, Left, Up, Up, Down, Left, Down, Left.

BURGER KING VINYL
At the title screen, Up, Up, Up, Up, Down, Up, Up, Left.

PERFORMANCE LEVEL 1
At the title screen, press ▣, ▣, ▣, ▣, Left, Left, Right, Up.

PERFORMANCE LEVEL 2
At the title screen, press ▣, ▣, ▣, ▣, Left, Right, Up, Down.

VISUAL LEVEL 1
At the title screen, press ▣, ▣, Up, Down, ▣, ▣, Up, Down.

VISUAL LEVEL 2
At the title screen, press ▣, ▣, Up, Down, ▣, Up, Up, Down.

NFL STREET

PASSWORDS
Enter the following as your user ID:

PASSWORD	EFFECT
Travel	All Fields
Classic	NFL Legends
Excellent	X-ecutioner Team
AW9378	Division All-Star Teams

NFL STREET 2

FUMBLE MODE
Enter GreasedPig as a code.

MAX CATCH
Enter MagnetHands as a code.

NO CHAINS MODE
Enter NoChains as a code.

NO FUMBLE MODE
Enter GlueHands as a code.

UNLIMITED TURBO
Enter NozBoost as a code.

EA FIELD
Enter EAField as a code.

AFC EAST ALL STARS
Enter EAASFSCT as a code.

AFC NORTH ALL STARS
Enter NAOFRCTH as a code.

AFC SOUTH ALL STARS
Enter SAOFUCTH as a code.

AFC WEST ALL STARS
Enter WAEFSCT as a code.

NFC EAST ALL STARS
Enter NNOFRCTH as a code.

NFC NORTH ALL STARS
Enter NNAS66784 as a code.

NFC SOUTH ALL STARS
Enter SNOFUCTH as a code.

NFC WEST ALL STARS
Enter ENASFSCT as a code.

TEAM REEBOK
Enter Reebok as a code.

TEAM XZIBIT
Enter TeamXzibit as a code.

PINBALL HALL OF FAME

CUSTOM BALLS OPTION
Enter BLZ as a code.

INFINITE LAST BALL OPTION
Enter INF as a code.

TILT OPTION
Enter NDG as a code.

PAYOUT MODE
Enter LAS as a code.

TOURNAMENT MODE
Enter TMA as a code.

GOTTLIEB FACTORY TOUR
Enter DGC as a code.

LOVE MACHINE
Enter LUV as a code.

PLAYBOY PINBALL TABLE
Enter PKR as a code.

XOLTEN FORTUNE MACHINE
Enter XTN as a code.

PITFALL: THE LOST EXPEDITION

PLAY AS NICOLE
At the Title screen, press and hold 🔲 +
🔲, then press Left, Up, Down, Up, ⬤,
Up, Up.

INFINITE WATER IN CANTEEN
At the Title screen, press and hold 🔲 +
🔲 then press Left, ⬤, ⬤, Down, ⬤,
✖, ⬤, ⬤.

HYPER PUNCH MODE
At the Title screen, press and hold 🔲
+ 🔲 then press Left, Right, ⬤, Up, ⬤,
Right, Left.

CLASSIC PITFALL
At the Title screen, press and hold 🔲 +
🔲 then press ⬤, ⬤, Left, Right, ⬤, ⬤,
✖, Up, ⬤.

CLASSIC PITFALL 2: LOST CAVERNS
At the Title screen, press and hold 🔲
+ 🔲 then press Left, Right, Left, Right,
⬤ (x3).

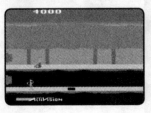

PRINCE OF PERSIA: THE SANDS OF TIME

CLASSIC PRINCE OF PERSIA
Start a new game and while on the balcony, hold L3 and enter ✖, ⬤, ▲, ⬤, ▲, ✖, ⬤, ⬤.

CLASSIC PASSWORDS

LEVEL	PASSWORD	LEVEL	PASSWORD
2	KIEJSC	8	SVZMSC
3	VNNNPC	9	DBJRPC
4	IYVPTC	10	MZFYSC
5	RWSWWC	11	BRAYQC
6	GONWUC	12	UUGTPC
7	DEFNUC	Jafar	LRARUC

PSYCHONAUTS

ALL POWERS
Hold L1 and R1 and press ⬤, ⬤, ▲, R2, L3, ▲.

9999 LIVES
Hold L1 and R1 and press L3, R2, R2, ⬤, ✖, R3.

9999 AMMO
Hold L1 and R1 and press R3, ✖, L3, L3, ▲, ⬤.

GLOBAL ITEMS
Hold L1 and R1 and press R3, ⬤, R2, R2, L3, ▲.

ALL POWERS UPGRADED
Hold L1 and R1 and press L3, R3, L3, R2, ⬤, R2.

10K ARROWHEADS
Hold L1 and R1 and press ✖, R3, R3, R2, ▲, ⬤.

R-TYPE FINAL

INVINCIBILITY
Pause the game, press and hold R2, then press Right, Right, Left, Right, Left, Left, Right, Left, R1, Up, Up, Down, Down, Up, Down, Up, Down, R1. Re-enter the code to disable it.

99.9% CHARGE DOSE
Pause the game, press and hold R2, then press R2, L2, Left, Right, Up, Down, Right, Left, Up, Down, ▲.

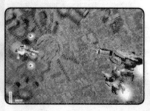

FULL BLUE POWER, MISSILES, AND BITS
Pause the game, press and hold R2, then press R2, L2, Left, Right, Up, Down, Right, Left, Up, Down, ⬤.

FULL RED POWER, MISSILES, AND BITS
Pause the game, press and hold R2, then press R2, L2, Left, Right, Up, Down, Right, Left, Up, Down, ⬤.

FULL YELLOW POWER, MISSILES, AND BITS
Pause the game, press and hold R2, then press R2, L2, Left, Right, Up, Down, Right, Left, Up, Down, ✖.

LADY LOVE SHIP (#3)
At the R Museum, enter 5270 0725 as a password.

STRIDER SHIP (#24)
At the R Museum, enter 2078 0278 as a password.

MR. HELI SHIP (#59)
At the R Museum, enter **1026 2001** as a password.

CURTAIN CALL SHIP (#100)
At the R Museum, enter **1009 9201** as a password.

RATCHET AND CLANK: UP YOUR ARSENAL

DUEL BLADE LASER SWORD
Pause the game and press ◉, ▣, ◉, ▣, Up, Down, Left, Left.

QWARK'S ALTERNATE COSTUME.
Start a game of Qwark Vid-Comic and press Up, Up, Down, Down, Left, Right, ◉, ◉, ▣.

PIRATE VS NINJA MINI GAME
At the Qwark Comics Issue select, press ▣ to bring up a password screen. Enter _MEGHAN_ as a password.

4-PLAYER BOMB MINIGAME
At the Qwark Comics Issue select, press ▣ to bring up a password screen. Enter YING_TZU as a password. Press Start, Select to return to Starship Phoenix.

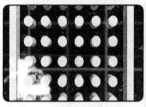

SLY 2: BAND OF THIEVES DEMO
At the Title screen, hold ▣ + ▣ + ▣ + ▣.

ROBOTECH: INVASION

Select Extras from the Options menu and enter the following codes:

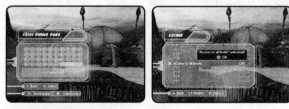

INVINCIBILITY
Enter supercyc.

UNLIMMITED AMMO
Enter trgrhpy.

ONE-HIT KILLS
Enter dustyayres.

ALL LEVELS
Enter reclamation.

LANCER'S MULTIPLAYER SKIN
Enter yllwfllw.

SCOTT BERNARDS MULTIPLAYER SKIN
Enter ltntcmdr.

RAND'S MULTIPLAYER SKIN
Enter kidgloves.

ROOK'S MULTIPLAYER SKIN
Enter blueangls.

ROBOTS

BIG HEAD
Pause the game and press Up, Down, Down, Up, Right, Right, Left, Right.

UNLIMITED HEALTH
Pause the game and press Up, Right, Down, Up, Left, Down, Right, Left.

UNLIMITED SCRAP
Pause the game and press Down, Down, Left, Up, Up, Right, Up, Down.

SAMURAI JACK: THE SHADOW OF AKU

MAXIMUM HEALTH
During a game, hold Left on the Left Analog Stick + Right on the Right Analog Stick, and press ✕, ●, ▲, ■.

MAXIMUM ZEN
During a game, hold Left on the Left Analog Stick + Right on the Right Analog Stick, and press ●, ✕, ■, ▲.

CRYSTAL SWORD
During a game, press Left on the Left Analog Stick Down + Up on the Right Analog Stick, then press ✕, ●, ■, ▲.

FIRE SWORD
During a game, press Down on the Left Analog Stick + Up on the Right Analog Stick, then press ■, ✕, ●, ▲.

LIGHTNING SWORD
During a game, press Down on the Left Analog Stick + Up on the Right Analog Stick, then press ●, ✕, ▲, ■.

SCALER

FULL HEALTH
Pause the game, select audio from the options and press R1, L1, R1, L1, ●, ●, ■, ■, R1, ■.

200,000 KLOKKIES
Pause the game, select audio from the options and press L1, L1, R1, R1, ●, ■, ●.

INFINITE ELECTRIC BOMBS
Pause the game, select audio from the options and press R1, R1, L1, L1, ●, ●, ■.

SD GUNDAM FORCE: SHOWDOWN!

BAKUNETSUMARU
In Kao Lyn's Lab, enter ⬤, ◉, ✕, ⬤, ◉, ✕, ⬤, ◉, ✕, ⬤, ◉, ◉.

CAPTAIN GUNDAM
In Kao Lyn's Lab, enter ◉, ⬛, ⬤, ✕, ✕, ⬤, ⬛, ◉, ⬤, ◉, ⬛, ✕.

ZERO THE WINGED KNIGHT
In Kao Lyn's Lab, enter ⬤, ⬤, ◉, ◉, ✕, ⬛, ✕, ⬛, ◉, ✕, ⬤, ⬛.

SECRET WEAPONS OVER NORMANDY

ALL PLANES, ENVIRONMENTS, AND MISSIONS
At the Main menu, press ⬛(x3), ◉(x3), ⬤, ⬛, then enter L2, R2, L2, R2.

ALL ENVIRONMENTS IN INSTANT ACTION
At the Main menu, press Up, Down, Left, Right, L1, R1, L1, R1.

INVINCIBILITY
At the Main menu, press Up, Down, Left, Right, Left, Left, Right, Right, L1, L1, R1, R1, L2, R2.

UNLIMITED AMMUNITION
At the Main menu, press Up, Right, Down, Left, Up, Right, Down, Left, L1, R1.

BIG HEADS
At the Main menu, press Right, Up, Left, Down, Right, Up, Left, Down, Right, L1, R1, L1, R1.

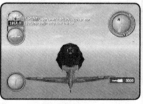

SEEK AND DESTROY

Enter the following passwords at the pink tank in the first town to get different bonuses:

1000 GOLD
At the pink tank, enter KWNOHIRO.

AIR GATLING GUN
At the pink tank, enter GSASINRI.

BOUND BOMB
At the pink tank, enter KKHWEEEE.

GRAND FLAG
At the pink tank, enter ODGRITRO.

SHAMAN KING: POWER OF SPIRIT

VERSUS MODE
Complete all 20 episodes in story mode.

MASKED MERIL IN VERSUS MODE
Press select on Meril

MATILDA IN VERSUS MODE
Press select on Kanna

MARION FAUNA IN VERSUS MODE
Press select on Matilda.

ZEKE ASAKURA IN VERSUS MODE
Press select on Yoh Asakura

SHARK TALE

REPLACE PEARLS WITH FISH KING COINS
During a level with Pearls, press Select, then hold ⬜ and press ⬤, ✖, ⬤(x3), ✖, ⬤, ⬤.
Release ⬜ to enable the cheat.

ATTACK
During a game, press Select, then hold ⬜ and press ⬤(x4), ✖, ⬤x4). Release ⬜ to enable the cheat.

CLAMS AND FAME
During a game, press Select, then hold ⬜ and press ⬤, ⬤, ✖, ✖, ⬤, ✖, ⬤, ⬤. Release ⬜ to enable the cheat.

SHREK 2

BONUS GAMES
Pause the game and select Scrapbook. Press Left, Up, ✖, ⬤, Left, Up, ✖, ⬤, Left, Up, ✖, ⬤, ⬛, ⬤, ⬛, ⬤, ⬛, ⬤. Exit the level and select Bonus to access the games.

CHAPTER SELECT
Pause the game and select Scrapbook. Press Left, Up, ✖, ⬤, Left, Up, ✖, ⬤, Left, Up, ✖, ⬤, Up, Up, Up, Up, Up. Exit the level and select Chapter Select to change chapters.

FULL HEALTH
Pause the game and select Scrapbook. Press Left, Up, ✖, ●, Left, Up, ✖, ●, Left, Up, ✖, ●, Up, Right, Down, Left, Up.

1,000 COINS
Pause the game and select Scrapbook. Press Left, Up, ✖, ●, Left, Up, ✖, ●, Left, Up, ✖, ● (x6).

THE SIMS BUSTIN' OUT

Pause the game, then enter the following codes. You must enter the Enable Cheats code first. After entering another code, select the gnome to access it.

ENABLE CHEATS
Press L2, L1, R1, R2, Left, ●. A gnome appears in your yard when the code is entered correctly.

FILL ALL MOTIVES
Press R2, R1, Left, ●, Up.

GIVE MONEY
Press L1, R2, Right, ●, ♦. Select the Gnome to give money.

UNLOCK ALL LOCATIONS
Press R3, ♦, ♦, L2, R1, R1.

UNLOCK ALL OBJECTS
Press R2, R2, Up, ▲, ♦.

UNLOCK ALL SKINS
Press L1, R2, ✖, ●, Up, Down.

UNLOCK ALL SOCIAL OPTIONS
Press L1, R1, Down, ✖, ♦, ♦.

SLY 2: BAND OF THIEVES

RESTART EPISODE
Pause the game and press Left, R1, Up, Down, Up, Left.

SKIP TO TUTORIAL
Pause the game and press Right, Left, Up, Up, Up, R1, Start.

SKIP TO EPISODE 1: THE BLACK CHATEAU
Pause the game and press Down, R1, Left, Right, R1, Down, Start.

SKIP TO EPISODE 2: A STARRY EYED ENCOUNTER
Pause the game and press R1, Left, Right, R1, Left, Down, Start.

SKIP TO EPISODE 3: THE PREDATOR AWAKES
Pause the game and press Up, Left, Right, Left, Down, Up, Start.

SKIP TO EPISODE 4: JAILBREAK
Pause the game and press Up, Right, Right, Up, Left, Left, Start.

SKIP TO EPISODE 5: A TANGLED WEB
Pause the game and press Left, ■, Down, Down, Up, Right, Start.

SKIP TO EPISODE 6: HE WHO TAMES THE IRON HORSE
Pause the game and press Down, Up, ■, ■, Left, Down, Start.

SKIP TO EPISODE 7: MENACE IN THE NORTH, EH?
Pause the game and press Left, Left, Left, Down, Down, ■, Start.

SKIP TO EPISODE 8: ANATOMY FOR DISASTER
Pause the game and press Down, Up, Left, Left, ■, Right, Start.

TOM GADGETPP
Pause the game and press Left, Left, Down, Right, Left, Right.

TIME RUSH GADGET
Pause the game and press Down, Down, Up, Down, Right, Left.

EPISODE EASTER EGGS
After each boss fight, leave the game on the Episode Menu of the level with the boss you just fought. If you don't touch a button or move to another menu for approximately eight to ten seconds, Carmelita's Badge will appear in the bottom left corner of the screen and start flashing for just a few seconds. As sonn as you see it, press the ● button to access a ssecret movie. There are a total of five secret clips, one for each level with a boss fight.

1: Episode 1: The Black Chateau—Sly 2: Band of Thieves promo trailer.

2: Episode 3: The Predator Awakes—MTV Lala promo.

3: Episode 5: A Tangled Web—Sly 2: Band of Thieves 15 second television commercial.

4: Episode 7: Menace in the North, Eh?—Sly Cooper "Making of" video.

5: Episode 8: Anatomy for Disaster—Credits Roll and "Where are they now" clips.

SONIC MEGA COLLECTION PLUS

Comix Zone

INVINCIBILITY
Select the jukebox from the options and play the following tracks in order: 3, 12, 17, 2, 2, 10, 2, 7, 7, 11.

STAGE SELECT
Select the jukebox from the options and play the following tracks in order: 14, 15, 18, 5, 13, 1, 3, 18, 15, 6.

Dr. Robotnik's Mean Bean Machine

EASY PASSWORDS

Continue a game with the following passwords:

LEVEL	PASSWORD
2	Red Bean, Red Bean, Red Bean, Has Bean
3	Clear Bean, Purple Bean, Clear Bean, Green Bean
4	Red Bean, Clear Bean, Has Bean, Yellow Bean
5	Clear Bean, Blue Bean, Blue Bean, Purple Bean
6	Clear Bean, Red Bean, Clear Bean, Purple Bean
7	Purple Bean, Yellow Bean, Red Bean, Blue bean
8	Yellow Bean, Green Bean, Purple Bean, Has Bean
9	Yellow Bean, Purple Bean, Has Bean, Blue Bean
10	Red Bean, Yellow Bean, Clear Bean, Has Bean
11	Green Bean, Purple Bean, Blue Bean, Clear Bean
12	Red Bean, Has Bean, Has Bean, Yellow Bean
13	Yellow Bean, Has Bean, Blue Bean, Blue Bean

NORMAL PASSWORDS

LEVEL	PASSWORD
2	Has Bean, Clear Bean, Yellow Bean, Yellow Bean
3	Blue Bean, Clear Bean, Red Bean, Yellow Bean
4	Yellow Bean, Blue Bean, Clear Bean, Purple Bean
5	Has Bean, Green Bean, Blue Bean, Yellow Bean
6	Green Bean, Purple Bean, Purple Bean, Yellow Bean
7	Purple Bean, Blue Bean, Green Bean, Has Bean
8	Green Bean, Has Bean, Clear Bean, Yellow Bean
9	Blue Bean, Purple Bean, Has Bean, Has Bean
10	Has Bean, Red Bean, Yellow Bean, Clear Bean
11	Clear Bean, Red Bean, Red Bean, Blue Bean
12	Green Bean, Green Bean, Clear Bean, Yellow Bean
13	Purple Bean, Yellow Bean, Has Bean, Clear Bean

HARD PASSWORDS

LEVEL	PASSWORD
2	Green Bean, Clear Bean, Yellow Bean, Yellow Bean
3	Yellow Bean, Clear Bean, Purple Bean, Clear Bean
4	Blue Bean, Green Bean, Clear Bean, Blue Bean
5	Red Bean, Purple Bean, Green Bean, Green Bean
6	Yellow Bean, Yellow Bean, Clear Bean, Green Bean
7	Purple Bean, Clear Bean, Blue Bean, Blue Bean
8	Clear Bean, Yellow Bean, Has Bean, Yellow Bean
9	Purple Bean, Blue Bean, Blue Bean, Green Bean
10	Clear Bean, Green Bean, Red Bean, Yellow Bean
11	Blue Bean, Yellow Bean, Yellow Bean, Has Bean
12	Green Bean, Clear Bean, Clear Bean, Blue bean
13	Has Bean, Clear Bean, Purple Bean, Has Bean

HARDEST PASSWORDS

LEVEL	PASSWORD
2	Blue Bean, Blue Bean, Green Bean, Yellow Bean
3	Green Bean, Yellow Bean, Green Bean, Clear Bean
4	Purple Bean, Purple Bean, Red Bean, Has Bean
5	Green Bean, Red Bean, Purple Bean, Blue Bean
6	Blue Bean, Purple Bean, Green Bean, Yellow Bean
7	Blue Bean, Purple Bean, Green Bean, Has Bean
8	Clear Bean, Purple Bean, Has Bean, Yellow Bean
9	Purple Bean, Green Bean, Has Bean, Clear Bean
10	Green Bean, Blue Bean, Yellow Bean, Has Bean
11	Green Bean, Purple Bean, Has Bean, Red Bean
12	Red Bean, Green Bean, Has Bean, Blue Bean
13	Red Bean, Red Bean, Clear Bean, Yellow Bean

RISTAR

LEVEL SELECT
Enter ILOVEU as a password.

FIGHT ONLY BOSSES
Enter MUSEUM as a password.

TIME ATTACK
Enter DOFEEL as a password.

TONE DEAF SOUNDS
Enter MAGURO as a password.

TRUE SIGHT
Enter MIEMIE as a password.

SUPER HARD
Enter SUPER as a password.

VERY HARD
Enter SUPERB as a password.

CANCEL CODES
Enter XXXXXX as a password.

SONIC THE HEDGEHOG

LEVEL SELECT
At the title screen press Up, Down, Right, Left. Hold ● and press Start.

SONIC THE HEDGEHOG 2

LEVEL SELECT
Select Sound Test from the Options. Play the following in this order: 19, 65, 09, 17. Exit the Options and immediately hold ● and press Start.

SONIC THE HEDGEHOG 3

LEVEL SELECT
While the game is loading, press Up, Up, Down, Down, Up, Up, Up, Up. Scroll down past Competition.

SONIC SPINBALL

ROUND SELECT
At the Options, press ●, Down, ✖, Down, ●, Down, ●, ✖, Up, ●, ●, Up, ✖, ●, Up.

Then, at the title screen, hold ● and press Start for Round 2. Hold ✖ and press Start for Round 3. Hold ● and press Start for Round 4.

SPIDER-MAN 2

TREYARCH PASSWORD
Start a New Game and enter HCRAYERT as your name. You will start at 44% complete, 201,000 Hero Points, some upgrades, and more.

SPONGEBOB SQUAREPANTS: THE MOVIE

SIX HEALTH SLOTS
Pause the game, hold R1 + L1 + R2 + L2 and press ●, ●, ●, ●, ●, ●, ●, ●.

ALL MOVES
Pause the game, hold R1 + L1 + R2 + L2 and press ●, ●, ●, ●, ●, ●, ●, ●.

ALL MOVES TO MACHO
Pause the game, hold R1 + L1 + R2 + L2 and press ●, ●, ●, ●, ●, ●, ●, ●.

DOUBLE MANLINESS POINTS
Pause the game, hold R1 + L1 + R2 + L2 and press ●, ●, ●, ●, ●, ●, ●, ●.

ALL UNKNOWN TASKS
Pause the game, hold R1 + L1 + R2 + L2 and press ●, ●, ●, ●, ●, ●, ●.

SPONGEBOB CAVEMAN
Pause the game, hold R1 + L1 + R2 + L2 and press ●, ●, ●, ●, ●, ●, ●, ●.

SPONGEBOB RIPPED SHORTS
Pause the game, hold R1 + L1 + R2 + L2 and press ●, ●, ●, ●, ●, ●.

PATRICK CAVEMAN
Pause the game, hold R1 + L1 + R2 + L2 and press ●, ●, ●, ●, ●, ●, ●, ●.

PATRICK GOOFY GOOBER
Pause the game, hold R1 + L1 + R2 + L2 and press ●, ●, ●, ●, ●, ●, ●.

STARSKY AND HUTCH

UNLOCK EVERYTHING

Enter VADKRAM as a profile name.

During a game, enter the following. The codes will last for 30 seconds.

CODE	EFFECT
▲, ■, ✖, ●(x2), ✖, ■, ▲.	Big Heads
Up, ✖, Down, ▲, Left, ●, Right, ■.	Funny Cars
Up, Right, Down, Left, ⊕, Left, Right, Left.	Invisible Car
Up, Up, Down, Down, ✖, ●, ▲, ■.	Low Rider
⬛, ⬛, Left, Right, ⊕(x4).	Monster Truck
▲, ■, ✖, ●, ●, ■, ▲	Normal View
Up, Up, Left, Left, ⬛, ⬛, ⬛, ⬛.	Trike Cam
⬛, ⬛, ⬛, ⬛, Left, Left, Up, Up.	Trippy Camera

STAR TREK: SHATTERED UNIVERSE

ALL MEDALS AND RANK AWARDED
At the Main menu, press ⬛, ⬛, ⬛, ●, ⬛, ▲, ⬛, Select.

ALL MISSIONS OPEN
At the Main menu, press ⬛, ⬛, ●, ■, ⬛, ⬛, ▲, Select.

ALL SHIPS UNLOCKED
At the Main menu, press ⬛, ■, ⬛, ■, ⬛, ⬛, ●, Select.

INVINCIBILITY
At the Main menu, press ⬛, ●, ⬛, ⬛, ▲, ●, ●, Select.

KOBAYASHI MARU OPEN
At the Main menu, press ⬛, ▲, ⬛, ⬛, ●, ▲, ⬛, Select.

STAR WARS: BATTLEFRONT

ALL MISSIONS
Select Historical Campaign, then press ■, ●, ■, ● at the Mission Select.

SMALL PEOPLE
Create a profile named Jub Jub.

STREET RACING SYNDICATE

At the Main menu, press Up, Down, Left, Right. This will bring up the code entry screen. Enter the following codes to enable these cheats:

MAZDA RX-8
Enter RENESIS

TOYOTA SUPRA 3.0L RZ
Enter SICKJZA

MITSUBISHI ECLIPSE GS-T
Enter IGOTGST

TOYOTA CELICA GT-S
Enter MYTCGTS

SUBARU IMPREZA S202 STI
Enter SICKGDB

POLICE CAR
Enter GOTPOPO

PAC MAN VINYL
Enter GORETRO

FREE CAR REPAIR
Enter FIXITUP. Your first car repair is free.

GET WARNING FOR FIRST 3 BUSTS
Enter LETMEGO. The first three times you are pulled over, you get a warning.

TEENAGE MUTANT NINJA TURTLES 2: BATTLE NEXUS

Select Password from the Options menu and enter the following. Hold 🔲 while selecting a turtle to get his New Nexus Turtle outfit.

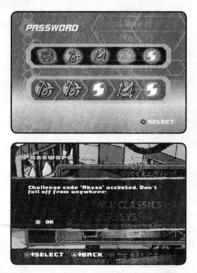

EFFECT	PASSWORD
Challenge Code Abyss	SDSDRLD
Challenge Code Endurance	MRMDRMD
Challenge Code Fatal Blow	LRSRDRD
Challenge Code Lose Shuriken	RLMRDSL
Challenge Code Nightmare	SLSDRDL
Challenge Code Poison	DRSLLSR
Challenge Code Super-Tough	RDSRMRL
Cheat Code All-You-Can-Throw Shuriken	RSRLRSM
Cheat Code Health	DSRDMRM
Cheat Code Mighty Turtle	LSDRRDR
Cheat Code Pizza Paradise	MRLMRMR
Cheat Code Self Recovery	DRMSRLR
Cheat Code Squeaking	MLDSRDM
Cheat Code Super Defense Power	LDRMRLM
Cheat Code Super Offense Power	SDLSRLL
Cheat Code Toddling	SSSMRDD
New Nexus Turtle outfit for Donatello	DSLRDRM
New Nexus Turtle outfit for Leonardo	LMRMDRD
New Nexus Turtle outfit for Michelangelo	MLMRDRM
New Nexus Turtle outfit for Raphael	RMSRMDR
Playmates added to Bonus Materials	SRMLDDR

TIGER WOODS PGA TOUR 2005

Select Passwords from the Options menu and enter the following codes to enable these cheats:

ALL GOLFERS AND COURSES
Enter THEGIANTOYSTER

ALL COURSES
Enter THEWORLDISYOURS

THE ROOF IN THE SKILLZONE GAME MODE
Enter NIGHTGOLFER

JUSTIN TIMBERLAKE
Enter THETENNESSEEKID

ARNOLD PALMER
Enter THEKING

BEN HOGAN
Enter PUREGOLF

SEVE BALLESTEROS
Enter THEMAGICIAN

JACK NICKLAUS
Enter GOLDENBEAR

GARY PLAYER
Enter BLACKKNIGHT

TIFFANY "TIFF" WILLIAMSON
Enter RICHGIRL

JEB "SHOOTER" MCGRAW
Enter SIXSHOOTER

HUNTER "STEELHEAD" ELMORE
Enter GREENCOLLAR

ALASTAIR" CAPTAIN" MCFADDEN
Enter NICESOCKS

BEV "BOOMER" BUOUCHIER
Enter THEBEEHIVE

ADRIANA "SUGAR" DULCE
Enter SOSWEET

APHRODITE PAPADAPOLUS
Enter TEMPTING

BILLY "BEAR" HIGHTOWER
Enter TOOTALL

KENDRA "SPIKE" LOVETTE
Enter ENGLISHPUNK

DION "DOUBLE D" DOUGLAS
Enter DDDOUGLAS

RAQUEL "ROCKY" ROGERS
Enter DOUBLER

BUNJIRO "BUD" TANAKA
Enter INTHEFAMILY

CEASAR "THE EMPEROR" ROSADO
Enter LANDOWNER

REGINALD "REG" WEATHERS
Enter REGGIE

THE HUSTLER
Enter ALTEREGO

SUNDAY TIGER WOODS
Enter NEWLEGEND

ADIDAS ITEMS
Enter 91treSTR

CALLAWAY ITEMS
Enter cgTR78qw

CLEVELAND ITEMS
Enter CL45etUB

MAXFLI ITEMS
Enter FDGH597i

NIKE ITEMS
Enter YJHk342B

ODYSSEY ITEMS
Enter kjnMR3qv

PING ITEMS
Enter R453DrTe

PRECEPT ITEMS
Enter BRi3498Z

TAG ITEMS
Enter cDsa2fgY

TOURSTAGE ITEMS
Enter TS345329

TOM AND JERRY IN WAR OF THE WHISKERS

INFINITE LIFE
During a game, press ✕, ●, ✕, ▲, ▲, ■, ●, ▲.

INFINITE AMMUNITION
During a game, press ●, ■, ●, ▲, ✕, ■, ✕, ✕.

ALL ARENAS
During a game, press ▲, ●, ▲, ▲, ✕, ■, ●, ■.

COSTUMES
During a game, press ●, ●, ✕, ■, ●, ▲, ✕, ●.

TONY HAWK'S UNDERGROUND 2

Select Cheat Codes from the Game Options and enter the following. For the cheats, pause the game and select Cheats to turn them on.

ALL LEVELS
Enter d3struct.

ALL SKATERS EXCEPT FOR SECRET SKATERS
Enter costars!.

THPS1 TONY HAWK AND ALL THUG2 MOVIES
Enter boxoffice.

NATAS KAUPAS
Enter oldskool

NIGEL BEAVERHAUSEN
Enter sellout

PHIL MARGERA
Enter aprilsman.

INFINITE RAIL CHEAT
Enter straightedge.

ALWAYS SPECIAL
Enter likepaulie.

SECRETS

Tony Hawk's Underground 2 has a wealth of unlockable skaters, videos, and levels for those who complete the various modes of play. Newcomers to the series will be happy to learn that some of the unlockables are earned through completion of Story Mode on the Easy and Normal difficulty settings, as well as the Sick setting. Similarly, veterans and completionists can take joy in knowing that completing both modes on the Sick setting also unlocks more skaters and that finding all of the gaps on all 15 levels unlocks the various cheat codes.

Rewards Table

GOAL ACHIEVED	LEVEL UNLOCKED	SKATERS UNLOCKED	MOVIES UNLOCKED
Complete Story Mode on "Easy"	Pro Skater	Shrek, Phil Margera, Peds Group A	World Destruction Tour
Complete Story Mode on "Normal"	Pro Skater	The Hand, Paulie, Peds Group B	World Destruction Tour
Complete Story Mode on "Sick"	Pro Skater	Call of Duty Soldier, Nigel, Peds Group C	World Destruction Tour
Complete Story Mode with 100%	N/A	Peds Group F	Pro Bails 2
Complete Classic Mode on "Normal"	The Triangle	Steve-O, THPS1 Tony, Peds Group D	Pro Bails 1
Complete Classic Mode on "Sick"	The Triangle	Jesse James, Natas Kaupas, Peds Group E	Pro Bails 1
Complete Classic Mode with 100%	N/A	Peds Group G	Neversoft Skates
Get all gaps on all 15 levels	N/A	Peds Group H	Cheat Codes
Complete Boston in Story Mode	N/A	Ben Franklin	N/A
Complete Barcelona in Story Mode	N/A	Bull Fighter	N/A
Complete Berlin in Story Mode	N/A	Graffiti Tagger	N/A
Complete Australia in Story Mode	N/A	Shrimp Vendor	N/A
Complete New Orleans in Story Mode	N/A	Jester	N/A
Complete Skatopia in Story Mode	N/A	Ryan Sheckler	N/A

TRANSFORMERS

ALL EXTRAS
Select Extras and press ●, ●, ●, ●, ●, ●, ▣, ▣.

INVINCIBILITY
Pause the game and press ▣, ●, ●, ▣, ▣, ▣, ▣, ▣.

STEALTH ENEMIES
Pause the game and press Left, Right, Left, ▣, ▣, ▣, Right, Right.

ONE-HIT KILLS
Pause the game and press ●, ◉, ●, ◉, ▣, ▣, ▣, ▣.

At the Autobot Headquarters menu, enter the following:

BIG HEAD CHEAT MODE
Press ◉(x3), ●, ▣(x3), ▣.

TURBO CHEAT MODE
Press ▣, ▣, ▣, ◉(x4), ▣.

UNLIMITED STEALTH
Press Up, Up, Down, Down, ▣, ▣, ▣, ▣.

UNLIMITED POWERLINK
Press Up, Down, Up, Down, ◉, ●, ●, ◉.

DISABLE MINI CON OVERLOAD
Press ▣, ▣, ▣, ▣, ▣, ▣, ◉, ◉.

Enter the following at the difficulty select screen:

ALASKA LEVEL COMPLETE
▣, ◉, ▣, ●, Left, Left, Right, Left

DEEP AMAZON LEVEL COMPLETE
Left, Right, Left, Left, Right, ▣, ▣, ◉

EARTH LEVEL COMPLETE
▣, ▣, ▣, ▣, ●, ◉, ●, ◉

MID ATLANTIC LEVEL COMPLETE
◉, ●, ◉, ●, Right, Left, Left, Right

STARSHIP LEVEL COMPLETE
Left, Left, Right, ◉, ◉, Right, Right, Left

AMAZON BOSS FIGHT
Left, Left, Right, ▣, ▣, Left, Left, Right

AMAZON LEVEL COMPLETE
▣, ▣, ▣, ●, ●, ◉, ▣, ▣

ANARCTICA BOSS FIGHT
▣, Left, ▣, Right, ●, ●, ◉, ◉

ANARCTICA LEVEL COMPLETE
▣, ▣, ▣, ▣, ▣, ▣, ▣, ▣

MID ATLANTIC BOSS FIGHT
▣, Left, Right, Right, Left, ▣, ▣, ▣

STARSHIP BOSS FIGHT
Right, Right, ●, ▣, ▣, ◉, Left, Left

TY THE TASMANIAN TIGER 2: BUSH RESCUE

ALL BUNYIP KEYS
During a game, press Start, ▲, Start, Start, ▲, ■, ◉, ■, ✕.

ALL FIRST-LEVEL RANGS
During a game, press Start, ▲, Start, Start, ▲, ◉, ■, ◉, ■.

ALL SECOND-LEVEL RANGS
During a game, press Start, ▲, Start, Start, ▲, ■, ◉, ■, ▲.

GET 100,000 OPALS
During a game, press Start, ▲, Start, Start, ▲, ◉, ✕, ◉, ✕.

HIGHLIGHT ALL COLLECTIBLES
During a game, press Start, ▲, Start, Start, ▲, Up, Down, Left, Right.

THE URBZ: SIMS IN THE CITY

CHEAT GNOME
During a game, press ◉, L1, L2, L2, L1.

JUMP AHEAD SIX HOURS
Enter the Cheat Gnome code and then press L2, R3, L3, L2, L1, L2.

ACQUIRE SKILL OBJECT
Enter the Cheat Gnome code and then press L1, L2, Right, ■, L3

MAX ARTISTIC SKILL
Enter the Cheat Gnome code and then press L3, R3, L1, L2, ◉

MAX MENTAL SKILL
Enter the Cheat Gnome code and then press L1, L2, ✕, ◉, Up

MAX PHYSICAL SKILL
Enter the Cheat Gnome code and then press L1, L1, Down, ✕, L3

ALL SOCIALS
Enter the Cheat Gnome code and then press L2, L2, UP, ▲, L3, X.

POWER SOCIALS
Enter the Cheat Gnome code and then press ▲, L2, L1, ✕, ■.

RAISE MOTIVES
Enter the Cheat Gnome code and then press L2, L1, L1, L2, Left, ◉.

DEVELOPMENT TEAM
Enter the Cheat Gnome code and then press Up, Down, ◉, Up, Down.

VAN HELSING

BONUS MOVIE 1
During a game, press Up, Down, Up, Down, Left, Left, Right, Right, L1, R1, L3, L1.

BONUS MOVIE 2
During a game, press Up, Right, Down, Left, Up, Left, Down, Right, Up, L1, L2, R3.

BONUS MOVIE 3
During a game, press L1, L2, L3, R1, R2, R3, L1, Up, Up, Down, Down, Select.

BONUS MOVIE 4
During a game, press Select, R3, L3, Select, L3, R3, Select, Left, Left, Up, Right, Right.

BONUS MOVIE 5
During a game, press L2, L2, L1, L1, Select, Select, R1, R1, R2, L2, R3, L3.

BONUS MOVIE 6
During a game, press ▣, ▣, ▣, ▣, ▣, ▣, ▣, ▣, Left, Right, Select, Select.

BONUS MOVIE 7
During a game, press ▣, Left, ▣, Right, ▣, Up, ▣, Down, ▣, Left, ▣, Right.

WORLD TOUR SOCCER 2005

ALL TEAMS AND STADIUMS
At the Main menu, press ▣, ▣, ▣, ▣, Up, Down, Left, Right.

QA LIVERPOOL, TIF OLDBOYS, TIF NEWBIES, AND TOUCHLINE TEAMS
At the Main menu, press Down, Right, ▣, ▣, Left, ▣.

TIMEWARP TEAMS
At the Main menu, press ▣, ▣, ▣, ▣, Up, ▣.

ALL BONUSES
At the Main menu, press ▣, ▣, ▣, ▣, Left, Up, Left, Down.

UNLIMITED MONEY
At the Main menu, press Right, Right, Left, Up (x3).

MORE TRANSFER MONEY
At the Main menu, press ▣, ▣, ▣, Down, Left, Right.

UNLIMITED SKILL FOR CUSTOM TEAMS
At the Main menu, press Up, Up, ▣, ▣, Up, ▣.

UNLIMITED TIF TOKENS
At the Main menu, press Up, Down, Up, Down, ▣, ▣, ▣, ▣, Up, Down, Up, Down.

ALL MOVIES
At the Main menu, press ▣, ▣ (x3), ▣, ▣.

FASTER ANNOUNCERS
At the Main menu, press ▣, ▣, ▣, ▣, ▣, ▣.

CLOWN SOUNDS
At the Main menu, press ▣, ▣, ▣, ▣, ▣, ▣.

FARM SOUNDS
At the Main menu, press ▣, ▣, ▣, Up, Down, Right.

CREDITS
At the Main menu, press ▣, ▣, ▣, ▣ (x3).

WRATH UNLEASHED

LARGE CHARACTERS
At the Title screen, press Left, ●, Up, ●, Right, ▲, Down, ▲.

DOUBLE HEALTH AND SPEED IN VERSUS AND TEAM FIGHTER MODES
At the Title screen, press Down, Down, Up, Down, Left, Right, Down, Up (x4), Right, Left, ●.

ALTERNATE CHARACTERS IN VERSUS MODE
At the Character Select screen, press ▣, ▣, Down, Down, ▣, Select, ▣, Select, ▣, ▣, ▣, ▣, ▣, Select.

ALTERNATE CHARACTERS IN TEAM FIGHTER MODE
At the Title screen, press ▣, ▣, Down, Down, ▣, Select, ▣, Select, ▣, ▣, ▣, ▣ (x3), Select. Press ▣ to for alternate characters.

XGRA: EXTREME-G RACING ASSOCIATION

ALL LEVELS OF RACING
Enter FREEPLAY at the Cheat Menu.

ALL TRACKS
Enter WIBBLE at the Cheat Menu.

O2 LIVERIED
Enter UCANDO at the Cheat Menu.

MESSAGE IN CREDITS
Enter MUNCHKIN, EDDROOLZ or EDDIEPOO at the Cheat Menu.

YS: THE ARK OF NAPISHTIM

How to Enter Cheat Codes

1. Select **New Game**.

2. Select **Cheat** to enter the Cheat Room.

3. To activate Cheat Mode, strike the colored crystals in this sequence:
   Red, Blue, Yellow, Red, Blue, Yellow. The sequence appears at the top
   left as you strike each crystal.

4. Perform a Downward Thrust strike on the center pedestal to
   complete the code and activate Cheat Mode.

5. You can now use the same method to enter one of the cheat codes
   listed below, then exit the Cheat Room.

6. The game selection buttons are now red. Games saved with the
   Cheat Mode enabled will appear in red.

CLEARFLAG
Hit the crystals in the following order: Red, Red, Red, Red, Blue, Blue, Blue, Blue, Yellow,
Yellow, Yellow, Yellow, Blue, Blue, Yellow, Yellow, Red, Red. Turns on all special features
normally available only after you've completed the game once—Nightmare Mode, Time
Attack, and Red Spirit Monuments. **Note:** When enabled, Red Spirit Monuments appear
after you reach Port Rimorge. They allow you to warp between the Rehdan Village and
Port Rimorge monuments to save travel time.

OPENING MOVIE WITH ENGLISH VOICE/ENGLISH TEXT
Hit the crystals in the following order: Blue, Blue, Yellow, Red.

OPENING MOVIE WITH ENGLISH VOICE/JAPANESE TEXT
Hit the crystals in the following order: Blue, Blue, Blue, Yellow, Red.

OPENING MOVIE WITH JAPANESE VOICE/ENGLISH TEXT
Hit the crystals in the following order: Blue, Blue, Blue, Blue, Yellow, Red.

OPENING MOVIE WITH JAPANESE VOICE/NO TEXT
Hit the crystals in the following order: Blue, Yellow, Red.

ALTERNATE OPENING MOVIE
Hit the crystals in the following order: Red, Blue, Red.

BEACH MOVIE WITH ENGLISH VOICE/ENGLISH TEXT
Hit the crystals in the following order: Blue, Blue, Red, Yellow

BEACH MOVIE WITH ENGLISH VOICE/JAPANESE TEXT
Hit the crystals in the following order: Blue, Blue, Blue, Red, Yellow.

BEACH MOVIE WITH JAPANESE VOICE/ENGLISH TEXT
Hit the crystals in the following order: Blue, Red, Red, Yellow.

BEACH MOVIE WITH JAPANESE VOICE/JAPANESE TEXT
Hit the crystals in the following order: Blue, Red, Yellow.

ROMUN FLEET ENTRANCE ANIME MOVIE
Hit the crystals in the following order: Blue, Red, Yellow, Red, Red, Yellow, Blue, Blue, Blue.

ROMUN FLEET ENTRANCE CG MOVIE
Hit the crystals in the following order: Blue, Red, Yellow, Red, Red, Yellow, Blue.

ROMUN FLEET DESTROYED ANIME MOVIE
Hit the crystals in the following order: Blue, Red, Yellow, Red, Red, Yellow, Red, Red, Red.

ROMUN FLEET DESTROYED CG MOVIE
Hit the crystals in the following order: Blue, Red, Yellow, Red, Red, Yellow, Red.

NAPISHTIM DESTROYED MOVIE WITH ENGLISH VOICE/ ENGLISH TEXT
Hit the crystals in the following order: Blue, Red, Yellow, Red, Red, Blue, Yellow, Yellow.

NAPISHTIM DESTROYED MOVIE WITH ENGLISH VOICE/ JAPANESE TEXT
Hit the crystals in the following order: Blue, Red, Yellow, Red, Red, Blue, Yellow, Yellow, Yellow.

NAPISHTIM DESTROYED MOVIE WITH JAPANESE VOICE/ ENGLISH TEXT
Hit the crystals in the following order: Blue, Red, Yellow, Red, Red, Blue, Yellow, Yellow, Yellow, Yellow.

NAPISHTIM DESTROYED MOVIE WITH JAPANESE VOICE/ JAPANESE TEXT
Hit the crystals in the following order: Blue, Red, Yellow, Red, Red, Blue, Yellow.

OLHA DEMO AFTER CLEARING TIME ATTACK ON HARD (JAPANESE)
Hit the crystals in the following order: Red, Red, Red, Red, Red, Blue, Blue, Blue, Yellow, Red, Blue, Blue, Yellow, Yellow, Yellow.

GAME IN JAPANESE
Hit the crystals in the following order: Yellow, Yellow, Red, Blue.

LEVEL 10
Hit the crystals in the following order: Red, Blue, Blue, Red, Red, Blue.

LEVEL 20
Hit the crystals in the following order: Red, Blue, Blue, Red, Red, Blue, Blue.

LEVEL 30
Hit the crystals in the following order: Red, Red, Blue, Blue, Red, Red, Blue, Blue.

LEVEL 40
Hit the crystals in the following order: Red, Red, Blue, Red, Red, Blue, Blue, Yellow.

LEVEL 60
Hit the crystals in the following order: Red, Red, Blue, Blue, Yellow, Yellow, Red, Red, Blue, Blue, Yellow, Yellow.

HALF PRICE ITEMS
Hit the crystals in the following order: Yellow, Yellow, Blue, Blue, Red, Red, Red, Yellow, Yellow, Yellow, Red, Red, Blue, Blue.

20 ITEM TOOL MAX INCREASE
Hit the crystals in the following order: Yellow, Yellow, Red, Red, Blue, Blue, Yellow, R.

MAXED OUT BLIRANTE SWORD
Hit the crystals in the following order: Blue, Blue, Yellow, Yellow, Yellow, Red, Blue, Red, Red, Red, Yellow, Yellow.

MAXED OUT LIVART SWORD
Hit the crystals in the following order: Blue, Blue, Blue, Yellow, Yellow, Red, Blue, Red, Red, Yellow, Yellow, Yellow.

MAXED OUT ERICCIL SWORD
Hit the crystals in the following order: Blue, Yellow, Yellow, Red, Red, Red, Blue, Blue, Red, Red, Yellow.

MAXED OUT ALL 3 SWORDS
Hit the crystals in the following order: Blue, Yellow, Red, Blue, Blue, Blue, Red, Red, Red, Yellow, Yellow, Yellow, Blue, Yellow, Red.

ALTERNATE ENDING MOVIES
PS2 Version Ending
In the Rehdan Village (Festival at Night): Toksa and Nahrya look toward Adol as he walks by.

At the Entrance of the Village: Isha runs toward the back, then returns.

On the Tres Mares: The cat is on the front of the ship.

PC (Anime) Version Ending
In the Rehdan Village (Festival at Night): Toksa and Nahrya do not turn to Adol.

At the Entrance of the Village: Isha continues on to the back

On the Tres Mares: The cat is sitting in a different part of the boat.

Ending Change Criteria
Direction Calman is facing: Faces Adol if he has gotten the Gold Locket.

Number of Pikkards: Found all four pikkards and returned them to Emilio.

YU-GI-OH! THE DUELIST OF THE ROSES

PASSWORDS

At the Build Deck screen, press R3 and enter the following passwords:

NUMBER	CARD	PASSWORD
#001	Seiyaryu	2H4D85J7
#019	Meteor Dragon	86985631
#042	Fairy's Gift	NVE7A3EZ
#043	Magician of Faith	GME1S3UM
#057	Left Arm of the Forbidden One	A5CF6HSH
#058	Exodia the Forbidden One	37689434
#146	Swordstalker	AHOPSHEB
#149	Greenkappa	YBJMCD6Z
#152	Tactical Warrior	054TC727
#191	Swordsman from a Foreign Land	CZ81UVGR
#478	Aqua Dragon	JXCB6FU7
#655	Ancient Tree of Enlightenment	EKJHQ109
#502	Barrel Dragon	GTJXSBJ7
#567	Beastking of the Swamps	QXNTQPAX
#291	Birdface	N54T4TY5
#348	Dragon Seeker	81EZCH8B
#372	Mystical Capture Chains	N1NDJMQ3
#458	Serpentine Princess	UMQ3WZUZ
#506	Blast Sphere	CZN5GD2X
#510	Robotic Knight	S5S7NKNH
#670	Fairy King Truesdale	YF07QVEZ
#674	Slate Warrior	73153736
#687	Mimicat	69YDQM85
#699	Dark Hole	UMJ10MQB
#702	Harpy's Feather Duster	8HJHQPNP
#732	Change of Heart	SBYDQM8B
#750	Earthshaker	Y34PN1SV
#758	Elf's Light	E5G3NRAD
#765	Horn of the Unicorn	S14FGKQ1
#794	Crush Card	SRA7L5YR
#806	Gravity Bind	OHNFG9WX
#814	Goblin Fan	92886423
#825	Royal Decree	8TETQHE1
#829	Mirror Wall	53297534

PSP™

The Games

DARKSTALKERS CHRONICLE: THE CHAOS TOWER

EX OPTION
At the main menu, hold L and select Option.

MARIONETTE IN ARCADE MODE
At the character select, highlight ? and press Start (x7) then press P or K.

OBORO BISHAMON IN ALL MODES
At the character select, highlight Bishamon, hold Start and press P or K.

SHADOW IN ARCADE MODE
At the character select, highlight ? and press Start (x5) then press P or K.

GRETZKY NHL

UNLOCK EVERYTHING
Enter SHOENLOC.

NFL STREET 2 UNLEASHED

Select Cheats and Codes from the Options and enter the following codes.

AFC EAST ALL STARS
Enter EAASFSCT as a code.

AFC NORTH ALL STARS
Enter NAOFRCTH as a code.

AFC SOUTH ALL STARS
Enter SAOFUCTH as a code.

AFC WEST ALL STARS
Enter WAEFSCT as a code.

NFC EAST ALL STARS
Enter NNOFRCTH as a code.

NFC NORTH ALL-STARS
Enter NNAS66784 as a code.

NFC SOUTH ALL STARS
Enter SNOFUCTH as a code.

NFC WEST ALL STARS
Enter ENASFSCT as a code.

REEBOK TEAM
Enter Reebok as a code.

EA FIELD
Enter EAField as a code.

GRIDIRON FIELD
Enter GRIDIRONPRK as a code.

BIG BALL
Enter BIGPig as a code.

MAX CATCH IN QUICK GAME
Enter MagnetHands as a code.

NO FUMBLE MODE IN QUICK GAME
Enter GlueHands as a code.

FUMBLE MODE IN QUICK GAME
Enter GreasedPig as a code.

UNLIMITED TURBO IN QUICK GAME
Enter NozBoost as a code.

NO FIRST DOWNS
Enter NoChains as a code.

SPIDER-MAN 2

LEVEL SELECT
Defeat the game with 100% complete. Start a new game with the name FLUWDEAR.

TIGER WOODS PGA TOUR

EMERALD DRAGON
Earn $1,000,000.

GREEK ISLES
Earn $1,500,000.

PARADISE COVER
Earn $2,000,000.

EA SPORTS FAVORITES
Earn $5,000,000

MEAN8TEEN
Earn $10,000,000.

FANTASY SPECIALS
Earn $15,000,000.

THE HUSTLER'S DREAM 18
Defeat The Hustler in Legend Tour.

TIGER'S DREAM 18
Defeat Tiger Woods in Legend Tour.

TONY HAWK'S UNDERGROUND 2 REMIX

PERFECT RAIL BALANCE
Select Cheat Codes from the Game Options and enter tightrope.

THPS1 TONY HAWK
Select Cheat Codes from the Game Options and enter birdman.

TWISTED METAL: HEAD-ON

These codes will not work for Multiplayer or Online modes.

HEALTH RECHARGED
Hold L + R and press ▲, ✖, ■, ●.

INFINITE AMMO
Hold L + R and press ▲, ▲, Down, Down, Left.

INVUNERABLE
Hold L + R and press Right, Left, Down, Up.

INFINITE WEAPONS
Hold L + R and press ▲, ▲, Down, Down.

KILLER WEAPONS
Hold L + R and press ✖, ✖, Up, Up.

MEGA GUNS
Hold L + R and press ✖, ▲, ✖, ▲

XBOX®

The Games

AMPED 2 171
APEX 172
THE BARD'S TALE 172
CRIMSON SKIES: HIGH ROAD TO REVENGE 172
DIGIMON RUMBLE ARENA 2 172
DUNGEONS AND DRAGONS HEROES 173
FIFA STREET 174
FUTURE TACTICS: THE UPRISING 174
GOBLIN COMMANDER: UNLEASH THE HORDE 174
GODZILLA: SAVE THE EARTH 176
GREG HASTINGS' TOURNAMENT PAINTBALL 177
THE INCREDIBLES 177
LEGO STAR WARS: THE VIDEO GAME 179
LMA MANAGER 2005 183
MADDEN NFL 2005 184
MAGIC: THE GATHERING - BATTLEGROUNDS 188
MIDNIGHT CLUB II 188
MIDNIGHT CLUB 3: DUB EDITION 188
MLB SLUGFEST: LOADED 189
MVP BASEBALL 2005 190
MX vs. ATV UNLEASHED 190
NASCAR 2005: CHASE FOR THE CUP 191
NBA BALLERS 192
NBA LIVE 2004 195
NBA STREET 2 197
NCAA FOOTBALL 2005 199
NEED FOR SPEED UNDERGROUND 2 200
NFL STREET 2 201
ODDWORLD STRANGER'S WRATH 201
OUTRUN 2 202
PANZER DRAGOON ORTA 203
PINBALL HALL OF FAME: THE GOTTLIEB COLLECTION 203

AMPED 2

Enter the following as a code. Cheats will disable saving.

LEVEL SELECT
Enter AllLevels.

ALL CHARACTERS
Enter AllMyPeeps.

PLAY AS BIGFOOT
Enter BrotherOfYeti.

PLAY AS BONES
Enter FunnyBone.

PLAY AS BUNNY
Enter Bunny.

PLAY AS FROSTY JACK
Enter FrostByte.

PLAY AS HERMIT JOE
Enter GetOffMyLand.

PLAY AS MOCAP MAN
Enter MoCapMan.

PLAY AS RADICAL
Enter Radical.

PLAY AS SHINY GAL
Enter MetalMaam.

PLAY AS STEEZY
Enter ChillinWSteezy.

PLAY AS YETI
Enter GoTeamYeti.

MAXIMUM STATS
Enter MaxSkills.

FAST BOARDER
Enter FastMove.

FAST SPINS
Enter SuperSpin.

ALL GRABS
Enter TrickedOut.

LOW GRAVITY
Enter LowGravity.

NO CRASHING
Enter DontCrash.

NO COLLISIONS
Enter NoCollisions.

ICY COURSES
Enter AllIce.

ALL MOVIES
Enter ShowRewards.

DISABLE CODES
Enter noCheats.

APEX

ALL TRACKS AND CIRCUITS
Start a new game in Dream mode and enter WORLD as a brand name.

ALL CONCEPT CARS
Start a new game in Dream mode and enter DREAMY as a brand name.

ALL PRODUCTION CARS
Start a new game in Dream mode and enter REALITY as a brand name.

THE BARD'S TALE

During a game, hold L + R and enter the following:

EVERYTHING ON (SILVER AND ADDERSTONES)
Up, Up, Down, Down, Left, Right, Left, Right

FULL HEALTH AND MANA
Left, Left, Right, Right, Up, Down, Up, Down

CAN'T BE HURT
Right, Left, Right, Left, Up, Down, Up, Down

CAN'T BE STRUCK
Left, Right, Left, Right, Up, Down, Up, Down

DAMAGE X100
Up, Down, Up, Down, Left, Right, Left, Right

CRIMSON SKIES: HIGH ROAD TO REVENGE

GOD MODE
During a game, press Y, A, X, B, Black.

$5,000
During a game, press A, Y, A, Y, Black.

10 TOKENS
During a game, press X, B, X, B, Black.

ALL PLANES
During a game, press Y, X, B, Y, Black.

SUPER PRIMARY WEAPON
During a game, press B, X, A, B, Black.

ULTRA HARD DIFFICULTY
During a game, press X, B, A, X, Black.

DIGIMON RUMBLE ARENA 2

ONE-HIT KILLS
At the title screen, press Right, Up, Left, Down, A, L + R.

EVOLVE ENERGY ITEM
At the title screen, press Y, Right, Down, B, L, A, R, A, Y.

EVOLVE METER ALWAYS FULL
At the title screen, press X, Right, A, Y, Left, B, L + R.

DUNGEONS AND DRAGONS HEROES

During a game, hold L and press A + Y. Now you can enter the following:

INVINCIBILITY
Enter PELOR.

NIGHTMARE DIFFICULTY SETTING
Enter MPS LABS.

UNLIMITED MYSTICAL WILL
Enter OBADHAI.

10,000 EXPERIENCE POINTS
Enter DSP633.

500,000 GOLD
Enter KNE637.

DEXTERITY UP 10
Enter YAN or ZXE053.

CONSTITUTION UP 10
Enter N STINE.

10 ANTI-VENOM
Enter SPINRAD.

10 BERSERK BREW
Enter THOMAS.

10 FASH FREEZE
Enter ESKO.

10 FIRE BOMB
Enter WEBER.

10 FIRE FLASK
Enter BROPHY.

10 FIREY OIL
Enter EHOFF.

10 GLOBE POTION
Enter WRight.

10 INSECT PLAGUE
Enter DERISO.

10 KEYS
Enter KEIDEL.

10 KEYS
Enter SNODGRASS.

10 LARGE HEALING POTIONS
Enter THOMPSON.

10 LARGE WILL POTIONS
Enter GEE.

10 MEDIUM POTIONS OF WILL
Enter LU.

10 POTIONS OF HASTE
Enter UHL.

10 PYROKINS
Enter SMITH.

10 ROD OF DESTRUCTION
Enter AUSTIN.

10 ROD OF FIRE
Enter DELUCIA.

10 ROD OF MIRACLES
Enter JARMAN.

10 ROD OF MISSILES
Enter MILLER.

10 ROD OF REFLECTION
Enter WHITTAKE.

10 ROD OF SHADOWS
Enter DINOLT.

10 THROWN AXE OF RUIN
Enter RAMERO.

10 THROWN DAGGERS OF STUNNING
Enter BELL.

10 THROWN DAGGERS
Enter MOREL.

10 THROWN HALCYON HAMMER
Enter PRASAD.

10 THROWN HAMMER
Enter BRATHWAI.

10 THROWN VIPER AXE
Enter FRAZIER.

10 THROWN VIPER AXE
Enter HOWARD.

10 THUDERSTONE
Enter ELSON.

10 TOME OF LESSONS
Enter PAQUIN.

10 TOME OF THE APPRENTICE
Enter BILGER.

10 TOME OF THE TEACHER
Enter MEFFORD.

10 TOMES OF THE MASTER
Enter SPANBURG.

10 WARP STONES
Enter HOPPENST.

10 HOLY WATER
Enter CRAWLEY.

VIEW CONCEPT ART
Enter CONCEPTS.

VIEW CREDITS
Enter CREDITS.

DISABLE CHEATS
Enter UNBUFF.

FIFA STREET

ALL CLOTHES
At the main menu, hold L + Y and press Right, Right, Left, Up (x3), Down, Left.

SMALL PLAYERS
Pause the game, hold L + Y and press Up, Left, Down, Down, Right, Down, Up, Left.

NORMAL SIZE PLAYERS
Pause the game, hold L + Y and press Right, Right, Up, Down, Down, Left, Right, Left.

FUTURE TACTICS: THE UPRISING

LEVEL SKIP
At the game select screen, press L, X, R, R, Black, X, L, R, Black..

UNLIMITED TURNS AND MOVEMENT
During a game, press Up, Up, Down, Down, Left, Right, Left, Left, R, L.

BIG HEADS
During a game, press Up, Left, Down, Left, Down, Up, Up, Left.

DISCO MODE
During a game, press L, Left, L, Left, R, Right, R, Right.

LOW GRAVITY
During a game, press Up (x6), Down, Right, Up.

GOBLIN COMMANDER: UNLEASH THE HORDE

During a game, hold R + L + Y + Down until a message appears on the right side of the screen. Re-enter the code to disable. Now enter the following codes. Again a message appears if entered correctly.

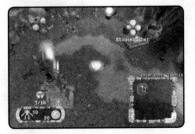

GOD MODE
Press R (x3), L (x3), R, L, Y, R.

AUTOMATIC WIN
Press R, R, L (x3), R, R, Y (x3).

ALL LEVEL ACCESS
Press Y (x3), L, R, L, L, R, L, R, R, L, R, L, L, R, L, R, L, L, R, L, R, L, L, R, L, R, R, Y (x3). Start up a Campaign to select a level.

DISABLE FOG OF WAR
Press R, L, R, R, L, L, Y, Y, L, R.

GAME SPEED X 1/2
Press L (x5), Y (x4), R.

GAME SPEED X 2
Press R (x5), L, Y, R (x3).

GOLD AND SOULS +1000
Press R, R, L, R, R, R, Y (x3), L, L.

GOLD +100
Press L, R (x4), L, Y, L (x3).

SOULS +100
Press R, L (x4), R, Y, R (x3).

GODZILLA: SAVE THE EARTH

CHEAT MENU
At the main menu, press and hold L, B, R in order, then let go of B, R, L in order. Now you can enter the following cheats.

ALL CITIES
Enter 659996.

ALL MONSTERS
Enter 525955.

UNLOCK CHALLENGES
Enter 975013.

HEALTH REGENERATES
Enter 536117.

ENERGY DOES NOT REGENERATE
Enter 122574.

INDESTRUCTIBLE BUILDINGS
Enter 812304.

100,000 POINTS
Enter 532459.

150,000 POINTS
Enter 667596.

200,000 POINTS
Enter 750330.

PLAYER 1: 4X DAMAGE
Enter 259565.

PLAYER 1: INFINITE ENERGY
Enter 819342.

PLAYER 1: INVISIBLE
Enter 531470.

PLAYER 1: INVULNERABLE
Enter 338592.

PLAYER 2: 4X DAMAGE
Enter 927281.

PLAYER 2: INFINITE ENERGY
Enter 324511.

PLAYER 2: INVISIBLE
Enter 118699.

PLAYER 2: INVULNERABLE
Enter 259333.

PLAYER 3: 4X DAMAGE
Enter 500494.

PLAYER 3: INFINITE ENERGY
Enter 651417.

PLAYER 3: INVISIBLE
Enter 507215.

PLAYER 3: INVULNERABLE
Enter 953598.

PLAYER 4: 4X DAMAGE
Enter 988551.

PLAYER 4: INFINITE ENERGY
Enter 456719.

PLAYER 4: INVISIBLE
Enter 198690.

PLAYER 4: INVULNERABLE
Enter 485542.

GALLERY
Enter 294206.

GODZILLA FINAL WARS
Enter 409014.

GREG HASTINGS' TOURNAMENT PAINTBALL

FLYING
During a game, hold Black + X + Right Trigger and press Up, Up, Down, Down, Right, Left, Down, Up.

THE INCREDIBLES

Pause the game, select Secrets and enter the following:

RESTORE SOME HEALTH
Enter UUDDLRLRBAS.

BIG HEADS
Enter EINSTEINIUM.

SMALL HEADS
Enter DEEVOLVE.

ONE HIT KILLS
Enter KRONOS.

INFINITE INCREDI-POWER FOR ELASTIGIRL
Enter FLEXIBLE.

INFINITE INCREDI-POWER FOR MR. INCREDIBLE
Enter SHOWTIME.

EYE LASER
Enter GAZERBEAM.

SUPER SPEED INCREDI-POWER
Enter DANIELTHEFLASH.

DESTROYS EVERYTHING
Enter SMARTBOMB.

FIRE TRAIL
Enter ATHLETESFOOT.

FASTER GAMEPLAY
Enter SASSMODE.

SLOW MOTION
Enter BWTHEMOVIE.

BRIGHT COLORS
Enter EMODE.

INVERT HORIZONTAL CAMERA CONTROL
Enter INVERTCAMERAX.

INVERT VERTICAL CAMERA CONTROL
Enter INVERTCAMERAY.

TOGGLE HUD
Enter BHUD.

WATCH HEAVY IRON STUDIOS INTRO
Enter HI.

CREDITS
Enter YOURNAMEINLIGHTS.

LEGO STAR WARS: THE VIDEO GAME

Extras

Pause the game and select Extras to toggle these cheats on and off.

INVINCIBILITY

At Dexter's Diner, select Enter Code and enter 4PR28U.

BIG BLASTERS

At Dexter's Diner, select Enter Code and enter IG72X4.

CLASSIC BLASTERS

At Dexter's Diner, select Enter Code and enter L449HD.

SILLY BLASTERS
At Dexter's Diner, select Enter Code and enter NR37W1.

BRUSHES
At Dexter's Diner, select Enter Code and enter SHRUB1.

TEA CUPS
At Dexter's Diner, select Enter Code and enter PUCEAT.

MINIKIT DETECTOR
At Dexter's Diner, select Enter Code and enter LD116B.

MOUSTACHES
At Dexter's Diner, select Enter Code and enter RP924W.

PURPLE
At Depxter's Diner, select Enter Code and enter YD77GC.

SILHOUETTES
At Dexter's Diner, select Enter Code and enter MS999Q.

Characters

These codes make each character available for purchase from Dexter's Diner.

BATTLE DROID
At Dexter's Diner, select Enter Code and enter 987UYR.

BATTLE DROID (COMMANDER)
At Dexter's Diner, select Enter Code and enter EN11K5.

BATTLE DROID (GEONOSIS)
At Dexter's Diner, select Enter Code and enter LK42U6.

BATTLE DROID (SECURITY)
At Dexter's Diner, select Enter Code and enter KF999A.

BOBA FETT
At Dexter's Diner, select Enter Code and enter LA811Y.

CLONE
At Dexter's Diner, select Enter Code and enter F8B4L6.

CLONE (EPISODE III)
At Dexter's Diner, select Enter Code and enter ER33JN.

CLONE (EPISODE III, PILOT)
At Dexter's Diner, select Enter Code and enter BHU72T.

CLONE (EPISODE III, SWAMP)
At Dexter's Diner, select Enter Code and enter N3T6P8.

CLONE (EPISODE III, WALKER)
At Dexter's Diner, select Enter Code and enter RS6E25.

COUNT DOOKU
At Dexter's Diner, select Enter Code and enter 14PGMN.

DARTH MAUL
At Dexter's Diner, select Enter Code and enter H35TUX.

DARTH SIDIOUS
At Dexter's Diner, select Enter Code and enter A32CAM.

DISGUISED CLONE
At Dexter's Diner, select Enter Code and enter VR832U.

DROIDEKA
At Dexter's Diner, select Enter Code and enter DH382U.

GENERAL GRIEVOUS
At Dexter's Diner, select Enter Code and enter SF321Y.

GEONOSIAN
At Dexter's Diner, select Enter Code and enter 19D7NB.

GRIEVOUS' BODYGUARD
At Dexter's Diner, select Enter Code and enter ZTY392.

GONK DROID
At Dexter's Diner, select Enter Code and enter U63B2A.

JANGO FETT
At Dexter's Diner, select Enter Code and enter PL47NH.

KI-ADI MUNDI
At Dexter's Diner, select Enter Code and enter DP55MV.

LUMINARA
At Dexter's Diner, select Enter Code and enter A725X4.

MACE WINDU (EPISODE III)
At Dexter's Diner, select Enter Code and enter MS952L.

PADMÉ
At Dexter's Diner, select Enter Code and enter 92UJ7D.

PK DROID
At Dexter's Diner, select Enter Code and enter R840JU.

PRINCESS LEIA
At Dexter's Diner, select Enter Code and enter BEQ82H.

REBEL TROOPER
At Dexter's Diner, select Enter Code and enter L54YUK.

ROYAL GUARD
At Dexter's Diner, select Enter Code and enter PP43JX.

SHAAK TI
At Dexter's Diner, select Enter Code and enter EUW862.

SUPER BATTLE DROID
At Dexter's Diner, select Enter Code and enter XZNR21.

LMA MANAGER 2005

QUICKER HEALING
Enter your name as LMA2005A.

£500,000,000
Enter your name as LMA2005B.

MOON BALL
Enter your name as LMA2005MA.

HELIUM SHOUTS
Enter your name as LMA2005MB.

BASS SHOUTS
Enter your name as LMA2005MC.

MADDEN NFL 2005

CHEAT CARDS

Select Madden Cards from the My Madden menu. Then, select Madden Codes and enter the following:

CHEAT	CODE
3rd Down, Opponent only get 3 downs to get a 1st	Z28X8K
5th Down, Get 5 downs to get a 1st Down	P66C4L
Aloha Stadium	G67F5X
Bingo!, Defensive interceptions increase by 75% for game	J33I8F
Da Bomb, Unlimited pass range	B61A8M
Da Boot, Unlimited field goal range	I76X3T
Extra Credit, Awards points for interceptions and sacks	M89S8G
First and Fifteen, your opponent must get 15 yards to get a 1st down	V65J8P
First and Five, 1st down yards are set to 5	O72E9B
Fumbilitis, Opponents fumbles increase by 75% for game	R14B8Z
Human Plow, Break tackle increases by 75% for game	L96J7P
Lame Duck, Opponent will throw lob passes	D57R5S
Mistake Free, Can't fumble or throw interceptions	X78P9Z
Mr. Mobility, Your QB can't get sacked	Y59R8R
Super Bowl XL	O85P6I
Super Bowl XLI	P48Z4D
Super Bowl XLII	T67R1O
Super Bowl XXXIX	D58F1B
Super Dive, Diving distance increases by 75%	D59K3Y
Tight Fit, Opponents uprights will be narrow	V34L6D
Unforced Errors, Opponent fumble ball when he jukes	L48G1E

CLASSIC TEAM CARDS

Select Madden Cards from the My Madden menu. Then, select Madden Codes and enter the following:

TEAM	CODE	TEAM	CODE
1958 Colts	P74X8J	1982 Redskins	F56D6V
1966 Packers	G49P7W	1983 Raiders	D23T8S
1968 Jets	C24W2A	1984 Dolphins	X23Z8H
1970 Browns	G12N1I	1985 Bears	F92M8M
1972 Dolphins	R79W6W	1986 Giants	K44F2Y
1974 Steelers	R12D9B	1988 49ers	F77R8H
1976 Raiders	P96Q8M	1990 Eagles	G95F2Q
1977 Broncos	O18T2A	1991 Lions	I89F4I
1978 Dolphins	G97U5X	1992 Cowboys	I44A1O
1980 Raiders	K71K4E	1993 Bills	Y66K3O
1981 Chargers	Y27N9A		

CHEERLEADER/PUMP UP THE CROWD CARDS

Select Madden Cards from the My Madden menu. Then, select Madden Codes and enter the following:

TEAM	CODE	TEAM	CODE
Patriots	O59P9C	Jaguars	K32C2A
49ers	X61T6L	Jets	S45W1M
Bengals	Y22S6G	Lions	C18F4G
Bills	F26S6X	Packers	K26Y4V
Broncos	B85U5C	Panthers	M66N4D
Browns	B65Q1L	Raiders	G92L2E
Buccaneers	Z55Z7S	Rams	W73B8X
Cardinals	Q91W5L	Ravens	P98T6C
Chargers	Q68S3F	Redskins	N19D6Q
Chiefs	T46M6T	Saints	R99G2F
Colts	M22Z6H	Seahawks	A35T8R
Cowboys	J84E3F	Steelers	C98I2V
Dolphins	E88T2J	Texans	R74G3W
Eagles	Q88P3Q	Titans	Q81V4N
Falcons	W86F3F	Vikings	E26H4L
Giants	L13Z9J		

GOLD PLAYER CARDS

Select Madden Cards from the My Madden menu. Then, select Madden Codes and enter the following:

PLAYER	CODE	PLAYER	CODE
Aaron Brooks	J95K1J	Andre Carter	V76E2Q
Aaron Glenn	Q48E9G	Andre Johnson	E34S1M
Adewale Ogunleye	C12E9E	Andy Reid	N44K1L
Ahman Green	T86L4C	Anquan Boldin	S32F7K
Al Wilson	G72G2R	Antonio Winfield	A12V7Z
Alan Faneca	U32S9C	Bill Cowher	S54T6U
Amani Toomer	Z75G6M	Brad Hopkins	P44A8B

PLAYER	CODE	PLAYER	CODE
Brett Farve	L61D7B	Edgerrin James	A75D7X
Brian Billick	L27C4K	Ed Reed	G18Q2B
Brian Dawkins	Y47B8Y	Eric Moulds	H34Z8K
Brian Simmons	S22M6A	Flozell Adams	R54T1O
Brian Urlacher	Z34J4U	Fred Taylor	I87X9Y
Brian Westbrook	V46I2I	Grant Wistrom	E46M4Y
Bubba Franks	U77F2W	Herman Edwards	O19T2T
Butch Davis	G77L6F	Hines Ward	M12B8F
Byron Leftwich	C55V5C	Jack Del Rio	J22P9I
Carson Palmer	O36V2H	Jake Delhomme	M86N9F
Casey Hampton	Z11P9T	Jake Plummer	N74P8X
Chad Johnson	R85S2A	Jamie Sharper	W27I7G
Chad Pennington	B64L2F	Jason Taylor	O33S6I
Champ Bailey	K89O9E	Jason Webster	M74B3E
Charles Woodson	F95N9J	Jeff Fisher	N62B6J
Chris Hovan	F14C6J	Jeff Garcia	H32H7B
Clinton Portis	Z28D2V	Jeremy Newberry	J77Y8C
Corey Simon	R11D7K	Jeremy Shockey	R34X5T
Courtney Brown	R42R75	Jerry Porter	F71Q9Z
Curtis Martin	K47X3G	Jerry Rice	K34F8S
Dallas Coach	O24U1Q	Jevon Kearse	A78B1C
Damien Woody	E57K9Y	Jim Haslett	G78R3W
Damien Woody	F78I1I	Jim Mora Jr.	N46C3M
Dante Hall	B23P8D	Jimmy Smith	I22J5W
Dat Nguyen	Q86I2S	Joe Horn	P91A1Q
Daunte Culpepper	O62O9K	John Fox	Q98R7Y
Dave Wannstedt	W73D7D	Jon Gruden	H61I8A
David Boston	A25I9F	Josh McCown	O33Y4X
David Carr	C16E2Q	Julian Peterson	M89J8A
Dennis Erickson	J83E3T	Julius Peppers	X5404Z
Dennis Green	C18J7T	Junior Seau	W26K6Q
Derrick Brooks	P93I9Q	Kabeer Gbaja-Biamala	U16I9Y
Derrick Mason	S98P3T	Keith Brooking	E12P4S
Deuce Mcallister	D11H4J	Keith Bulluck	M63N6V
Dexter Coakley	L35K1A	Kendrell Bell	T96C7J
Dexter Jackson	G16B2I	Kevan Barlow	A23T5E
Dick Vermeil	F68V1W	Kevin Mawee	L76E6S
Dom Capers	B97I6R	Kris Jenkins	W63O3K
Domanick Davis	L58S3J	Kyle Boller	A72F9X
Donie Edwards	E18Y5Z	Kyle Turley	Y46A8V
Donovin Darius	Q11T7T	Ladainian Tomlinson	M64D4E
Donovon Mcnabb	T98J1I	Lavar Arrington	F19Q8W
Donte Stallworth	R75W3M	Laveranues Coles	R98I5S
Drew Bledsoe	W73M3E	Lawyer Milloy	M37Y5B
Dre'Bly	Z68W8J	La'roi Glover	K24L9K
Dwight Freeney	G76U2L	Lee Suggs	Z94X6Q

PLAYER	CODE	PLAYER	CODE
Leonard Davis	H14M2V	Rich Gannon	Q69I1Y
Lovie Smith	L38V3A	Richard Seymore	L69T4T
Marc Bulger	U66B4S	Ricky Williams	P19V1N
Marcel Shipp	R42X2L	Rod Smith	V22C4L
Marcus Stroud	E56I50	Rodney Harrison	08413J
Marcus Trufant	R46T5U	Rondel Barber	J72X8W
Mark Brunell	B66D9J	Roy Williams	J76C6F
Marshell Faulk	U76G1U	Rudi Johnson	W26J6H
Marty Booker	P51U4B	Sam Madison	Z87T5C
Marty Booker	H19Q2O	Samari Rolle	C69H4Z
Marty Shottenheimer	D96A7S	Santana Moss	H79E5B
Marvin Harrison	T11E80	Seattle Coach	V58U4Y
Marvin Lewis	P24S4H	Shaun Alexander	C95Z4P
Matt Hasselback	R68D5F	Shaun Ellis	Z54F2B
Michael Bennett	W81W2J	Shaun Rogers	J97X8M
Michael Strahan	O66T6K	Shawn Springs	J95K1J
Michael Vick	H67B1F	Simeon Rice	S62F9T
Mike Alstott	D89F6W	Stephen Davis	E39X9L
Mike Brown	F12J8N	Steve Mariucci	V74Q3N
Mike Martz	R64A8E	Steve Mcnair	S36T1I
Mike Mularkey	C56D6E	Steve Smith	W91O2O
Mike Rucker	K89O6S	T.J. Duckett	P67E1I
Mike Shanahan	H15L5Y	Takeo Spikes	B83A6C
Mike Sherman	F84X6K	Tedy Bruschi	K28Q3P
Mike Tice	Y31T6Y	Terence Newman	W57Y5P
New England Coach	N24L4Z	Terrell Suggs	V71A9Q
Nick Bernett	X95I7S	Tiki Barber	T43A2V
Norv Turner	F24K1M	Todd Heap	H19M1G
Olin Kreutz	R17R20	Tom Brady	X22V7E
Orlando Pace	U42U9U	Tom Coughlin	S71D6H
Patrick Surtain	H58T9X	Tony Dungy	Y96R8V
Peerless Price	X75V6K	Tony Gonzalez	N46E9N
Peter Warrick	D86P8O	Torry Holt	W96U7E
Peyton Manning	L48H4U	Travis Henry	F36M2Q
Plaxico Burress	K18P6J	Trent Green	Y46M4S
Priest Holmes	X91N1L	Ty Law	F13W1Z
Quentin Jammer	V55S3Q	Walter Jones	G57P1P
Randy Moss	W79U7X	Washington Coach	W63V9L
Ray Lewis	B94X6V	Will Shields	B52S8A
Reggie Wayne	R29S8C	Zach Thomas	U63I3H
Rex Grossman	C46P2A		

MAGIC: THE GATHERING - BATTLEGROUNDS

ALL QUESTS
At the quest select, press L + R, Down, Up, press the Left thumbstick, White, Up, Right, Left, Down, L + R.

SECRET LEVEL
At the arena select, press L + R, Left, Up, X, Up, Right, Y, L + R.

ALL DUELISTS
At the character select, press L + R, Down, Up, X, White, Up, X, Black, Up, X, L + R.

MIDNIGHT CLUB II

Select Cheat Codes from the Options and enter the following:

ALL VEHICLES
Enter **hotwired**.

ALL CITIES IN ARCADE MODE
Enter **theworldismine**.

WEAPONS
Enter **lovenotwar**. Press the Left Thumbstick and White to fire.

UNLIMITED NITROUS IN ARCADE MODE
Enter **zoomzoom4**.

ALL CAR ABILITIES
Enter **greasemonkey**.

EXTRA STAT
Enter **bigbrother**.

GAME SPEED
Enter one of the following, 0 is slowest, 9 is fastest.

howfastcanitbe0	howfastcanitbe5
howfastcanitbe1	howfastcanitbe6
howfastcanitbe2	howfastcanitbe7
howfastcanitbe3	howfastcanitbe8
howfastcanitbe4	howfastcanitbe9

CHANGE DIFFICULTY
0 is easiest, 9 is hardest.

howhardcanitbe0	howhardcanitbe5
howhardcanitbe1	howhardcanitbe6
howhardcanitbe2	howhardcanitbe7
howhardcanitbe3	howhardcanitbe8
howhardcanitbe4	howhardcanitbe9

MIDNIGHT CLUB 3: DUB EDITION

ALL CITIES AND RACES IN ARCADE MODE
Select Cheat Codes from the Options and enter urbansprawl, roadtrip or crosscountry.

NO DAMAGE
Select Cheat Codes from the Options and enter ontheroad.

ARGO SPECIAL MOVE
Select Cheat Codes from the Options and enter dfens.

ROAR SPECIAL MOVE
Select Cheat Codes from the Options and enter Rjnr.

ZONE SPECIAL MOVE
Select Cheat Codes from the Options and enter allin.

ADD $1 TO CAREER MONEY
Select Cheat Codes from the Options and enter kubmir.

SUBTRACT $1 OF CAREER MONEY
Select Cheat Codes from the Options and enter rimbuk.

BUNNY HEAD
Select Cheat Codes from the Options and enter getheadl.

CHROME HEAD
Select Cheat Codes from the Options and enter haveyouseenthisboy.

FLAMING HEAD
Select Cheat Codes from the Options and enter trythisathome.

SNOWMAN HEAD
Select Cheat Codes from the Options and enter getheadm.

PUMPKIN HEAD
Select Cheat Codes from the Options and enter getheadk.

YELLOW SMILE HEAD
Select Cheat Codes from the Options and enter getheadj.

MLB SLUGFEST: LOADED

CHEATS
At the Match-Up screen, press X, Y, and B to enter the following codes, then press the appropriate direction. For example, for 16" Softball press X (x2), Y (x4), B (x2), then press Down.

CODE	ENTER	CODE	ENTER
Bone Bat	0-0-1 Up	Eagle Team	2-1-2 Right
Blade Bat	0-0-2 Up	Evil Clown Team	2-1-1 Down
Ice Bat	0-0-3 Up	Gladiator Team	1-1-3 Down
Log Bat	0-0-4 Up	Horse Team	2-1-1 Right
Spike Bat	0-0-5 Up	Lion Team	2-2-0 Right
Whiffle Bat	0-0-4 Right	Minotaur Team	1-1-0 Down
Max Batting	3-0-0 Left	Napalitano Team	2-3-2 Down
Max Power	0-3-0 Left	Olshan Team	2-2-2 Down
Max Speed	0-0-3 Left	Pinto Team	2-1-0 Right
Unlimited Turbo	4-4-4 Down	Rivera Team	2-2-2 Up
Extra Time After Plays	1-2-3 Left	Rodeo Clown Team	1-3-2 Down
Little League Mode	1-0-1 Down	Scorpion Team	1-1-2 Down
16" Softball	2-4-2 Down	Terry Fitzgerald Team	3-3-3 Right
Rubber Bball	2-4-2 Up	Todd McFarlane Team	2-2-2 Right
Tiny Head	2-0-0 Left	Atlantis Stadium	3-2-1 Left
Big Head	2-0-0 Right	Coliseum Stadium	3-3-3 Up
Alien Team	2-3-1 Down	Empire Park Stadium	3-2-1 Right
Bobblehead Team	1-3-3 Down	Forbidden City Stadium	3-3-3 Left
Casey team	2-3-3 Down	Midway Park Stadium	3-2-1 Down
Dolphin Team	1-0-2 Down	Monument Stadium	3-3-3 Down
Dwarf Team	1-0-3 Down	Rocket Park Stadium	3-2-1 Up

MVP BASEBALL 2005

ALL STADIUMS, PLAYERS, UNIFORMS AND REWARDS
Create a player named Katie Roy.

GOOD HITTER WITH BIG BAT
Create a player named Isaiah Paterson, Jacob Paterson or Keegan Paterson.

BONE-SCALING CHEAT
Create a player named Kenny Lee.

MX vs. ATV UNLEASHED

UNLOCK EVERYTHING
Select Cheat Codes from the Options and enter TOOLAZY.

1,000,000 POINTS
Select Cheat Codes from the Options and enter BROKEASAJOKE. After entering the code, press Done multiple times for more points.

ALL PRO RIDERS
Select Cheat Codes from the Options and enter WANNABE.

ALL GEAR
Select Cheat Codes from the Options and enter WARDROBE.

50CC BIKE CLASS
Select Cheat Codes from the Options and enter MINIMOTO.

ALL MACHINES
Select Cheat Codes from the Options and enter LEADFOOT.

ALL FREESTYLE TRACKS
Select Cheat Codes from the Options and enter HUCKIT.

NASCAR 2005: CHASE FOR THE CUP

DALE EARNHARDT

At the Edit Driver screen, enter The Intimidator as your name.

$10,000,000

At the Edit Driver screen, enter Walmart NASCAR as your name.

2,000,000 PRESTIGE POINTS

At the Edit Driver screen, enter You TheMan as your name.

EXCLUSIVE TRACK

At the Edit Driver screen, enter Walmart Exclusive as your name.

ALL THUNDER PLATES

At the Edit Driver screen, enter Open Sesame as your name.

NBA BALLERS

VERSUS SCREEN CHEATS

You can enter the following codes at the Vs screen. The X button corresponds to the first number in the code, the Y is the second number, and the B button corresponds to the last number. Press the D-pad in any direction to enter the code.

EFFECT	CODE
Tournament Mode	0 1 1
Big Head	1 3 4
Baby Ballers	4 2 3
Kid Ballers	4 3 3
Young Ballers1	4 4 3
Paper Ballers	3 5 4
Alternate Gear	1 2 3
Expanded Move Set	5 1 2
Super Push	3 1 5
Super Block Ability	1 2 4
Great Handles	3 3 2
Unlimited Juice	7 6 3
Super Steals	2 1 5
Perfect Free Throws	3 2 7
Speedy Players	2 1 3
Better Free Throws	3 1 7
Fire Ability	7 2 2
Hotspot Ability	6 2 7
Back-In Ability	1 2 2
2x Juice Replenish	4 3 1
Stunt Ability	3 7 4
Pass 2 Friend Ability	5 3 6
Alley-Oop Ability	7 2 5
Put Back Ability	3 1 3
Legal Goal Tending	7 5 6
Show Shot Percentage	0 1 2
R2R Mode	0 0 8
Play As Coach	5 6 7
Play As Agent	5 5 7
Play As Secretary	5 4 7
Play As BiznezMan-A	5 3 7
Play As BiznezMan-B	5 2 7
Play As Afro Man	5 1 7
Super Back-Ins	2 3 5
Half House	3 6 7
Random Moves	3 0 0
Pygmy	4 2 5

PHRASE-OLOGY CODES/ALTERNATE GEAR

Select Phrase-ology from the Inside Stuff option and enter the following codes to unlock the Alternate Gear for the corresponding player.

PLAYER	PHRASE
Allan Houston	KNICKER BOCKER PLEASE
Allen Iverson	KILLER CROSSOVER
Alonzo Mourning	ZO
Amare Stoudemire	RISING SUN
Antoine Walker	BALL HAWK
Baron Davis	STYLIN' & PROFILIN'
Ben Wallace	RADIO CONTROLLED CARS
Bill Russell	CELTICS DYNASTY
Bill Walton	TOWERS OF POWER
Carmelo Anthony	NEW TO THE GAME
Chris Webber	24 SECONDS
Clyde Drexler	CLYDE THE GLIDE
Darko Milicic	NBA FASTBREAK
Darryl Dawkins	RIM WRECKER
Dejaun Wagner	NBA HANGTIME
Dikembe Mutumbo	IN THE PAINT
Dominique Wilkins	DUNK FEST
Eddie Jones	BALLER UPRISING
Elton Brand	REBOUND
Emanuel Ginobili	MANU
Gary Payton	GLOVE IS IN LA
George Gervin	THE ICE MAN COMETH
Grant Hill	GONE GOLD WITH IT
Isiah Thomas	TRUE BALLER
Jalen Rose	BRING IT
Jason Kidd	PASS THE ROCK
Jason Terry	BALL ABOVE ALL
Jason Williams	GIVE AND GO
Jerry Stackhouse	STOP DROP AND ROLL
John Stockton	COURT VISION
Julius Irving	ONE ON ONE
Karl Malone	SPECIAL DELIVERY
Kenyon Martin	TO THE HOLE
Kevin Garnett	BOSS HOSS
Kevin McHale	HOLLA BACK
Kobe Bryant	JAPANESE STEAK
Larry Bird	HOOSIER
Latrell Sprewell	SPREE
Lebron James	KING JAMES
Magic Johnson	LAKER LEGENDS
Michael Finley	STUDENT OF THE GAME
Mike Bibby	DREAMS & SCHEMES
Moses Malone	LOST FREESTYLE FILES

PLAYER	PHRASE
Nate "Tiny" Archibald	NATE THE SKATE
Nene Hilario	RAGS TO RICHES
Oscar Robertson	AINT NO THING
Pau Gasol	POW POW POW
Paul Pierce	CELTICS SUPREME
Pete Maravich	PISTOL PETE
Rashard Lewis	FAST FORWARD
Rasheed Wallace	BRING Down THE HOUSE
Ray Allen	ALL STAR
Reggie Miller	FROM DownTOWN
Richard Hamilton	RIP
Robert Parish	THE CHIEF
Scottie Pippen	PLAYMAKER
Shaquille O'Neal	DIESEL RULES THE PAINT
Shawn Marion	MAKE YOUR MARK
Stephon Marbury	PLATINUM PLAYA
Steve Francis	ANKLE BREAKER
Steve Francis	RISING STAR
Steve Nash	HAIR CANADA
Tim Duncan	MAKE IT TAKE IT
Tony Parker	RUN AND SHOOT
Tracy McGrady	LIVING LIKE A BALLER
Vince Carter	CHECK MY CRIB
Wally Szczerbiak	WORLD
Walt Frazier	PENETRATE AND PERPETRATE
Wes Unseld	OLD SCHOOL
Willis Reed	HALL OF FAME
Wilt Chamberlain	WILT THE STILT
Yao Ming	CENTER OF ATTENTION

CRIBS

Select Phrase-ology from the Inside Stuff option and enter the following to unlock player cribs.

CRIB	PHRASE
Allen Iverson's Recording Studio	THE ANSWER
Karl Malone's Devonshire Estate	ICE HOUSE
Kobe Bryant's Italian Estate	EURO CRIB
Scottie Pippen's Yacht	NICE YACHT
Yao Ming's Childhood Grade School	PREP SCHOOL

OTHER PHRASE-OLOGY CODES

Select Phrase-ology from the Inside Stuff option and enter the following to unlock that bonus.

BONUS	PHRASE
All Players, Alternate Gear, and Cinemas	NBA BALLERS TRUE PLAYA
Special Movie #1	JUICE HOUSE
Special Movie #2	NBA SHOWTIME
Special Movie #3	NBA BALLERS RULES
Special Movie #4	HATCHET MAN
Special Movie #5	SLAM IT
Special Shoe #2	COLD STREAK
Special Shoe #3	LOST YA SHOES

NBA LIVE 2004

Create a player with the following last name:

ALEKSANDER PAVLOVIC
Enter **WHSUCPOI**.

ANDREAS GLYNIADAKIS
Enter **POCKDLEK**.

CARLOS DELFINO
Enter **SDFGURKL**.

JAMES LANG
Enter **NBVKSMCN**.

JERMAINE DUPRI
Enter **SOSODEF**.

KYLE KORVER
Enter **OEISNDLA**.

MALICK BADIANE
Enter **SKENXIDO**.

MARIO AUSTIN
Enter **POSNEGHX**.

MATT BONNER
Enter **BBVDKCVM**.

NEDZAD SINANOVIC
Enter **ZXDSDRKE**.

PACCELIS MORLENDE
Enter **QWPOASZX**.

REMON VAN DE HARE
Enter **ITNVCJSD**.

RICK RICKERT
Enter **POILKJMN**.

SANI BECIROVIC
Enter **ZXCCVDRI**.

SOFOKLIS SCHORTSANITIS
Enter **IOUBFDCJ**.

SZYMON SZEWCZYK
Enter **POIOIJIS**.

TOMMY SMITH
Enter **XCFWQASE**.

XUE YUYANG
Enter **WMZKCOI**.

Select NBA Codes from the My NBA LIVE option and enter the following:

15,000 NBA STORE POINTS
Enter **87843H5F9P**.

ALL HARDWOOD CLASSIC JERSEYS
Enter **725JKUpLMM**.

ALL NBA GEAR
Enter **ERT9976KJ3**.

ALL TEAM GEAR
Enter **YREY5625WQ**.

ALL SHOES
Enter **POUY985GY5**.

UNLOCK SHOES

Select My NBA Live and enter the following NBA Codes to unlock the different shoes:

SHOES	CODE
Air Bounds (black/white/blue)	7YSS0292KE
Air Bounds (white/black)	JA807YAM20
Air Bounds (white/green)	84HHST61QI
Air Flight 89 (black/white)	FG874JND84
Air Flight 89 (white/black)	63RBVC7423
Air Flight 89 (white/red)	GF9845JHR4
Air Flightposite 2 (blue/gray)	2389JASE3E
Air Flightposite (white/black/gray)	74FDH7K94S
Air Flightposite (white/black)	6HJ874SFJ7
Air Flightposite (yellow/black/white)	MN54BV45C2
Air Flightposite 2 (blue/gray)	RB84UJHAS2
Air Flightposite 2 (blue/gray)	2389JASE3E
Air Foamposite 1 (blue)	OP5465UX12
Air Foamposite 1 (white/black/red)	D0D843HH7F
Air Foamposite Pro (blue/black)	DG56TRF446
Air Foamposite Pro (black/gray)	3245AFSD45
Air Foamposite Pro (red/black)	DSAKF38422
Air Force Max (black)	F84N845H92
Air Force Max (white/black/blue)	985KJF98KJ
Air Force Max (white/red)	8734HU8FFF
Air Hyperflight (white)	14TGU7DEWC
Air Hyperflight (black/white)	WW44YHU592
Air Hyperflight (blue/white)	A0K374HF8S
Air Hyperflight (yellow/black)	JCX93LSS88
Air Jordan 11 (black/red/white)	GF64H76ZX5

SHOES	CODE
Air Jordan 11 (black/varsity royal/white)	HJ987RTGFA
Air Jordan 11 (cool grey)	GF75HG6332
Air Jordan 11 (white)	HG76HN765S
Air Jordan 11 (white/black)	A2S35TH7H6
Air Jordan 3 (white)	G9845HJ8F4
Air Jordan 3 (white/clay)	435SGF555Y
Air Jordan 3 (white/fire red)	RE6556TT90
Air Jordan 3 (white/true blue)	FDS9D74J4F
Air Jordan 3 (black/white/gray)	CVJ554TJ58
Air Max2 CB (black/white)	87HZXGFIU8
Air Max2 CB (white/red)	4545GFKJIU
Air Max2 Uptempo (black/white/blue)	NF8745J87F
Air Max Elite (black)	A4CD54T7TD
Air Max Elite (white/black)	966ERTFG65
Air Max Elite (white/blue)	FD9KN48FJF
Air Zoom Flight (gray/white)	367UEY6SN
Air Zoom Flight (white/blue)	92387HDO77
Zoom Generation (white/black/red)	23LBJNUMB1
Zoom Generation (black/red/white)	LBJ23CAVS1
Nike Blazer (khaki)	W3R57U9NB2
Nike Blazer (tan/white/blue)	DCT5YHMU90
Nike Blazer (white/orange/blue)	4G66JU99XS
Nike Blazer (black)	XCV6456NNL
Nike Shox BB4 (black)	WE424TY563
Nike Shox BB4 (white/black)	23ERT85LP9
Nike Shox BB4 (white/light purple)	668YYTRB12
Nike Shox BB4 (white/red)	424TREU777
Nike Shox VCIII (black)	SDFH764FJU
Nike Shox VCIII (white/black/red)	5JHD367JJT

NBA STREET VOL. 2

Select Pick Up Game, hold L and enter the following codes when "Enter cheat codes now" appears at the bottom of the screen:

UNLIMITED TURBO
Press X, X, Y, Y.

ABA BALL
Press B, X, B, X.

WNBA BALL
Press B, Y, Y, B.

NO DISPLAY BARS
Press X, B (x3).

ALL JERSEYS
Press B, Y, X, X.

ALL COURTS
Press X, Y, Y, X.

ST. LUNATICS TEAM AND ALL STREET LEGENDS
Press X, Y, B, Y.

ALL NBA LEGENDS
Press B, Y, Y, X.

CLASSIC MICHAEL JORDAN
Press B, Y, B, B.

EXPLOSIVE RIMS
Press B (x3), Y.

SMALL PLAYERS
Press Y, Y, B, X.

BIG HEADS
Press B, X, X, B.

NO COUNTERS
Press Y, Y, B, B.

BALL TRAILS
Press Y, Y, Y, X.

ALL QUICKS
Press Y, B, Y, X.

EASY SHOTS
Press Y, B, X, Y.

HARD SHOTS
Press Y, X, B, Y.

NCAA FOOTBALL 2005

PENNANT CODES
At the Pennant Collection, press the Right thumbstick and enter the following:

CODE	EFFECT
EA Sports	Cuffed Cheat
Thanks	1st and 15
Sic Em	Baylor powerup
For	Blink (ball spotted short)
Registering	Boing (dropped passes)
Tiburon	Crossed The Line
Oskee Wow	Illinois Team Boost
Hike	Jumbalaya
Home Field	Molasses Cheat
Elite 11	QB Dud
NCAA	Stiffed
Football	Take Your Time
Fight	Texas Tech Team Boost
2005	Thread The Needle
Tech Triumph	Virginia Tech Team Boost
Blitz	What a Hit
Fumble	2003 All-Americans
Roll Tide	Alabama All-time
Raising Cane	Miami All-time
Go Blue	Michigan All-time
Hail State	Mississippi State All-time
Go Big Red	Nebraska All-time
Rah Rah	North Carolina All-time
We Are	Penn State All-time
Death Valley	Clemson All-time
Glory	Colorado All-time
Victory	Kansas State All-time
Quack Attack	Oregon All-time
Fight On	USC All-time
Bow Down	Washington All-time
Bear Down	Arizona mascot team
WooPigSooie	Arkansas All-time
War Eagle	Auburn All-time
U Rah Rah	Badgers All-time
Great To Be	Florida All-time
Great To Be	Florida All-time
Uprising	Florida State All-time
Hunker Down	Georgia All-time
On Iowa	Iowa All-time
Geaux Tigers	LSU All-time
Golden Domer	Notre Dame All-time
Boomer	Oklahoma All-time

CODE	EFFECT
Go Pokes	Oklahoma State All-time
Lets Go Pitt	Pittsburgh All-time
Boiler Up	Purdue All-time
Orange Crush	Syracuse All-time
Big Orange	Tennessee All-time
Gig Em	Texas A&M All-time
Hook Em	Texas All-time
Mighty	UCLA All-time
Killer Bucks	Ohio State All-time
Killer Nuts	Ohio State All-time
Wahoos	Virginia All-time
Ramblinwreck	Georgia Tech Mascot Team
Red And Gold	Iowa St. Mascot Team
Rock Chalk	Kansas Mascot Team
On On UK	Kentucky Mascot Team
Go Green	Michigan State Mascot Team
Rah Rah Rah	Minnesota Mascot Team
Mizzou Rah	Missouri Mascot Team
Go Pack	NC State Mascot Team
Go Cats	NU Mascot Team
Hotty Totty	Ole Miss Mascot Team
Hail WV	West Virginia Mascot Team
Go Deacs Go	Wake Forest Mascot Team
All Hail	WSU Mascot Team

NEED FOR SPEED UNDERGROUND 2

ALL CIRCUIT TRACKS
At the main menu, press Down, R, R, R, Black, Black, Black, X.

BEST BUY VINYL
At the main menu, press Up, Down, Up, Down, Down, Up, Right, Left.

BURGER KING VINYL
At the main menu, press Up, Up, Up, Up, Down, Up, Up, Left.

H2 CAPONE
At the main menu, press Up, Left, Up, Up, Down, Left, Down, Left.

NISSIAN SKYLINE
At the main menu, press Down, Down, L, White, L, White, L, Down.

LEVEL 1 PERFORMANCE PARTS
At the main menu, press L, R, L, R, Left, Left, Right, Up.

LEVEL 2 PERFORMANCE PARTS
At the main menu, press R, R, L, R, Left, Right, Up, Down.

LEVEL 1 VISUAL PARTS
At the main menu, press R, R, Up, Down, L, L, Up, Down.

LEVEL 2 VISUAL PARTS
At the main menu, press L, R, Up, Down, L, Up, Up, Down.

NFL STREET 2

FUMBLE MODE IN QUICK GAME
Enter GreasedPig as a code.

MAX CATCH IN QUICK GAME
Enter MagnetHands as a code.

NO CHAINS MODE IN QUICK GAME
Enter NoChains as a code.

NO FUMBLE MODE IN QUICK GAME
Enter GlueHands as a code.

UNLIMITED TURBO IN QUICK GAME
Enter NozBoost as a code.

EA FIELD
Enter EAField as a code.

AFC EAST ALL-STARS
Enter EAASFSCT as a code.p

AFC NORTH ALL-STARS
Enter NAOFRCTH as a code.

AFC SOUTH ALL-STARS
Enter SAOFUCTH as a code.

AFC WEST ALL-STARS
Enter WAEFSCT as a code.

NFC EAST ALL-STARS
Enter NNOFRCTH as a code.

NFC NORTH ALL-STARS
Enter NNAS66784 as a code.

NFC SOUTH ALL-STARS
Enter SNOFUCTH as a code.

NFC WEST ALL-STARS
Enter ENASFSCT as a code.

TEAM REEBOK
Enter Reebok as a code.

TEAM XZIBIT
Enter TeamXzibit as a code.

ODDWORLD STRANGER'S WRATH

LEVEL SELECT
Start a new game and enter ©@®& as a name.

CHEAT MODE
During a game, insert a controller in port 2. Remove the controller and press X, X, Y, Y, B, B, A, A on controller 1.

INVINCIBILITY
After entering the above Cheat Mode code, press X, Y, A, B, X, Y.

$1000
After entering the above Cheat Mode code, press Left Thumbstick, Left Thumbstick, Right Thumbstick, Right Thumbstick, Left Thumbstick, Left Thumbstick, Right Thumbstick, Right Thumbstick. You can repeat this code as much as you wish.

OUTRUN 2

Select OutRun Challenge and go to the Gallery. Choose Enter Code and enter the following:

ALL CARS
Enter DREAMING.

ALL MISSION STAGES
Enter THEJOURNEY.

BONUS TRACKS
Enter TIMELESS.

REVERSE TRACKS
Enter DESREVER.

ALL MUSIC
Enter RADIOSEGA.

ORIGINAL OUTRUN
Enter NINETEEN86.

ALL CARDS
Enter BIRTHDAY.

PANZER DRAGOON ORTA

ORIGINAL PANZER DRAGOON CODES
The following codes are for the Original Panzer Dragoon. Unlock it first by beating the game or playing for 5 hours. Once unlocked enter the following codes at the main menu of the original Panzer Dragoon.

INVINCIBLE
Enter L, L, R, R, Up, Down, Left, Right.

STAGE SELECT
Enter Up, Up, Down, Down, Left, Right, Left, Right, X, Y, White.

PLAY STAGE 0
Enter Up, Up, Up, Down, Down, Down, Left, Right, Left, Right, Left, Right, L, R.

ROLLING MODE
Enter Up, Right, Down, Left, Up, Right, Down, Left, Up, Right, Down, Left, Up, Right, Down, Left.

WIZARD MODE (FASTER GAME PLAY)
Enter L, R, L, R, Up, Down, Up, Down, Left, Right.

WATCH ENDING
Enter Up, Up, Down, Up, Right, Right, Left, Right, Down, Down, Up, Down, Left, Left, Right, Left.

PINBALL HALL OF FAME: THE GOTTLIEB COLLECTION

LOVE METER MACHINE
Enter LUV at the codes screen.

PLAYBOY MACHINE
Enter PKR at the codes screen.

XOLTEN MACHINE
Enter XTN at the codes screen.

FACTORY TOUR
Enter DGC at the codes screen

PAYOUT MODE
Enter LAS at the codes screen.

PRINCE OF PERSIA: THE SANDS OF TIME

CLASSIC PRINCE OF PERSIA ROOM
Start a new game. On the balcony, press Left Thumbstick, A, X, Y, B, Y, A, X, B.

CLASSIC PASSWORDS

LEVEL	PASSWORD
Level 2	KIEJSC
Level 3	VNNNPC
Level 4	IYVPTC
Level 5	RWSWWC
Level 6	GONWUC
Level 7	DEFNUC
Level 8	SVZMSC
Level 9	DBJRPC
Level 10	MZFYSC
Level 11	BRAYQC
Level 12	UUGTPC
Battle with Jafar	LRARUC

PSYCHONAUTS

ALL POWERS
During a game, hold Left Trigger + Right Trigger and press B, B, Y, White, Left Thumbstick, Y.

9999 LIVES
During a game, hold Left Trigger + Right Trigger and press Left Thumbstick, White, White, B, A, Right Thumbstick.

9999 AMMO (BLAST, CONFUSION)
During a game, hold Left Trigger + Right Trigger and press Right Thumbstick, A, Left Thumbstick, Left Thumbstick, Y, B.

GLOBAL ITEMS (NO PSI-BALL COLORIZER, NO DREAM FLUFFS)
During a game, hold Left Trigger + Right Trigger and press Right Thumbstick, B, White, White, Left Thumbstick, Y.

ALL POWERS UPGRADED (MAX RANK)
During a game, hold Left Trigger + Right Trigger and press Left Thumbstick, Right Thumbstick, Left Thumbstick, White, B, White.

9999 ARROWHEADS
During a game, hold Left Trigger + Right Trigger and press A, Right Thumbstick, Right Thumbstick, White, Y, X.

RALLISPORT CHALLENGE 2

CARS AND TRACKS SET 1
Select Credits from the Options and press Down, Left, Down, Right, Up, Up.

CARS AND TRACKS SET 2
Select Credits from the Options and press Left, Left, Down, Down, Right, Right.

CARS AND TRACKS SET 3
Select Credits from the Options and press Down, Down, Left, Left, Up, Down.

CARS AND TRACKS SET 4
Select Credits from the Options and press Right, Down, Right, Down, Left, Up.

CARS AND TRACKS SET 5
Select Credits from the Options and press Left, Left, Right, Right, Down, Left.

CARS AND TRACKS SET 6
Select Credits from the Options and press Right, Up, Up, Up, Down, Left.

CARS AND TRACKS SET 7
Select Credits from the Options and press Left, Left, Left, Up, Up, Right.

CARS AND TRACKS SET 8
Select Credits from the Options and press Right, Up, Left, Up, Down, Right.

CARS AND TRACKS SET 9
Select Credits from the Options and press Down, Up, Down, Left, Left, Down.

CARS AND TRACKS SET 10
Select Credits from the Options and press Up, Up, Down, Down, Left, Right.

ROBOTECH: INVASION

Select Extras from the Options menu and enter the following codes:

INVINCIBILITY
Enter supercyc.

UNLIMMITED AMMO
Enter trgrhpy.

1 HIT KILLS
Enter dustyayres.

ACCESS TO ALL LEVELS
Enter reclamation.

LANCER'S MULTIPLAYER SKIN
Enter yllwfllw.

SCOTT BERNARD'S MULTIPLAYER SKIN
Enter ltntcmdr.

RAND'S MULTIPLAYER SKIN
Enter kidgloves.

ROOK'S MULTIPLAYER SKIN
Enter blueangls.

ROBOTS

BIG HEAD FOR RODNEY
Pause the game and press Up, Down, Down, Up, Right, Right, Left, Right.

UNLIMITED HEALTH
Pause the game and press Up, Right, Down, Up, Left, Down, Right, Left.

UNLIMITED SCRAP
Pause the game and press Down, Down, Left, Up, Up, Right, Up, Down.

SCALER

FULL HEALTH
Pause the game, select audio from the options and press R, L, R, L, Y, Y, X, X, R, X.

200,000 KLOKKIES
Pause the game, select audio from the options and press L, L, R, R, Y, X, Y.

INFINITE ELECTRIC BOMBS
Pause the game, select audio from the options and press R, R, L, L, Y, Y, X.

SECRET WEAPONS OVER NORMANDY

ALL PLANES, ENVIRONMENTS, GALLERY AND MISSIONS
At the main menu, press Y, Y, Y, X, X, X, L, R, Black, Black, White White.

ALL ENVIRONMENTS IN INSTANT ACTION
At the main menu, press Up, Down, Left, Right, L, R, L, R.

INVINCIBILITY
At the main menu, press Up, Down, Left, Right, Left, Left, Right, Right, L, L, R, R, White, Black.

UNLIMITED AMMUNITION
At the main menu, press Up, Right, Down, Left, Up, Right, Down, Left, L Button, R Button.

BIG HEADS
At the main menu, press Right, Up, Left, Down, Right, Up, Left, Down, Right, L Button, R Button, L Button, R Button.

SHREK 2

BONUS GAMES
Pause the game and select Scrapbook. Press Left, Up, A, B, Left, Up, A, B, Left, Up, A, B, X, B, X, B, X, B. Exit the level and select Bonus to access the games.

CHAPTER SELECT
Pause the game and select Scrapbook. Press Left, Up, A, B, Left, Up, A, B, Left, Up, A, B, Up (x5). Exit the level and select Chapter Select to change chapters.

FULL HEALTH
Pause the game and select Scrapbook. Press Left, A, B, Circle, Left, A, B, Circle, Left, A, B, Up, Right, Down, Left, Up.

1,000 COINS
Pause the game and select Scrapbook. Press Left, Up, A, B, Left, Up, A, B, Left, Up, A, B (x6).

THE SIMS BUSTIN' OUT

Pause the game, then enter the following codes. You must enter the Enable Cheats code first. After entering another code, select the gnome to access it.

ENABLE CHEATS
Press R, L, Down, Black, Left, B. A gnome appears in your yard when the code is entered correctly.

GIVE MONEY
Press L, Black, Right, X, Left. Select the Gnome to give money.

UNLOCK ALL LOCATIONS
Press Black, Down, R, L, Down, Y.

UNLOCK ALL OBJECTS
Press Black, Up, Y, Down, R.

UNLOCK ALL SOCIAL OPTIONS
Press L, R, A, Down, Black.

SONIC HEROES

METAL CHARACTERS IN 2-PLAYER
After selecting a level in 2-Player, hold A + Y.

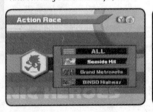 

SONIC MEGA COLLECTION PLUS

Comix Zone

INVINCIBILITY
Select the jukebox from the options and play the following tracks in order: 3, 12, 17, 2, 2, 10, 2, 7, 7, 11.

STAGE SELECT
Select the jukebox from the options and play the following tracks in order: 14, 15, 18, 5, 13, 1, 3, 18, 15, 6.

Dr. Robotnik's Mean Bean Machine

EASY PASSWORDS

Continue a game with the following passwords:

LEVEL	PASSWORD
2	Red Bean, Red Bean, Red Bean, Has Bean
3	Clear Bean, Purple Bean, Clear Bean, Green Bean
4	Red Bean, Clear Bean, Has Bean, Yellow Bean
5	Clear Bean, Blue Bean, Blue Bean, Purple Bean
6	Clear Bean, Red Bean, Clear Bean, Purple Bean
7	Purple Bean, Yellow Bean, Red Bean, Blue Bean
8	Yellow Bean, Green Bean, Purple Bean, Has Bean

LEVEL	PASSWORD
9	Yellow Bean, Purple Bean, Has Bean, Blue Bean
10	Red Bean, Yellow Bean, Clear Bean, Has Bean
11	Green Bean, Purple Bean, Blue Bean, Clear Bean
12	Red Bean, Has Bean, Has Bean, Yellow Bean
13	Yellow Bean, Has Bean, Blue Bean, Blue Bean

NORMAL PASSWORDS

LEVEL	PASSWORD
2	Has Bean, Clear Bean, Yellow Bean, Yellow Bean
3	Blue Bean, Clear Bean, Red Bean, Yellow Bean
4	Yellow Bean, Blue Bean, Clear Bean, Purple Bean
5	Has Bean, Green Bean, Blue Bean, Yellow Bean
6	Green Bean, Purple Bean, Purple Bean, Yellow Bean
7	Purple Bean, Blue Bean, Green Bean, Has Bean
8	Green Bean, Has Bean, Clear Bean, Yellow Bean
9	Blue Bean, Purple Bean, Has Bean, Has Bean
10	Has Bean, Red Bean, Yellow Bean, Clear Bean
11	Clear Bean, Red Bean, Red Bean, Blue Bean
12	Green Bean, Green Bean, Clear Bean, Yellow Bean
13	Purple Bean, Yellow Bean, Has Bean, Clear Bean

HARD PASSWORDS

LEVEL	PASSWORD
2	Green Bean, Clear Bean, Yellow Bean, Yellow Bean
3	Yellow Bean, Clear Bean, Purple Bean, Clear Bean
4	Blue Bean, Green Bean, Clear Bean, Blue Bean
5	Red Bean, Purple Bean, Green Bean, Green Bean
6	Yellow Bean, Yellow Bean, Clear Bean, Green Bean
7	Purple Bean, Clear Bean, Blue Bean, Blue Bean
8	Clear Bean, Yellow Bean, Has Bean, Yellow Bean
9	Purple Bean, Blue Bean, Blue Bean, Green Bean
10	Clear Bean, Green Bean, Red Bean, Yellow Bean
11	Blue Bean, Yellow Bean, Yellow Bean, Has Bean
12	Green Bean, Clear Bean, Clear Bean, Blue bean
13	Has Bean, Clear Bean, Purple Bean, Has Bean

HARDEST PASSWORDS

LEVEL	PASSWORD
2	Blue Bean, Blue Bean, Green Bean, Yellow Bean
3	Green Bean, Yellow Bean, Green Bean, Clear Bean
4	Purple Bean, Purple Bean, Red Bean, Has Bean
5	Green Bean, Red Bean, Purple Bean, Blue Bean
6	Blue Bean, Purple Bean, Green Bean, Yellow Bean
7	Blue Bean, Purple Bean, Green Bean, Has Bean
8	Clear Bean, Purple Bean, Has Bean, Yellow Bean
9	Purple Bean, Green Bean, Has Bean, Clear Bean

LEVEL	PASSWORD
10	Green Bean, Blue Bean, Yellow Bean, Has Bean
11	Green Bean, Purple Bean, Has Bean, Red Bean
12	Red Bean, Green Bean, Has Bean, Blue Bean
13	Red Bean, Red Bean, Clear Bean, Yellow Bean

RISTAR

LEVEL SELECT
Enter ILOVEU as a password.

FIGHT ONLY BOSSES
Enter MUSEUM as a password.

TIME ATTACK
Enter DOFEEL as a password.

TONE DEAF SOUNDS
Enter MAGURO as a password.

TRUE SIGHT
Enter MIEMIE as a password.

SUPER HARD
Enter SUPER as a password.

VERY HARD
Enter SUPERB as a password.

CANCEL CODES
Enter XXXXXX as a password.

SPIDER-MAN 2

TREYARCH PASSWORD
Start a New Game and enter HCRAYERT as your name. You will start at 44% complete, 201,
000 Hero Points, some upgrades and more.

SPIKEOUT: BATTLE STREET

EASY MODE
Die twice and continue to find a new Easy Mode option.

SPONGEBOB SQUAREPANTS: THE MOVIE

ALL HEALTH
Pause the game, hold L + R and press Y, Y, Y, Y, X, Y, X, X, Y.

ALL TASKS
Pause the game, hold L + R and press Y, X, Y, Y, X, Y, X, X.

ALL MOVES
Pause the game, hold L + R and press X, X, Y, X, Y, Y, X, X.

ALL MOVES TO MACHO
Pause the game, hold L + R and press X, X, Y, X, Y, Y, X, Y.

SONGEBOB CAVEMAN COSTUME
Pause the game, hold L + R and press X, X, X, X, Y, X, X, X.

SPONGEBOB RIPPED SHORTS COSTUME
Pause the game, hold L + R and press X, X, X, X, Y, X, X, Y.

PATRICK CAVEMAN COSTUME
Pause the game, hold L + R and press X, X, X, X, Y, X, Y, Y.

PATRICK GOOFY GOOBER COSTUME
Pause the game, hold L + R and press X, X, X, X, Y, X, Y, X.

SPY VS. SPY

ALL STORY MODE LEVELS
Select Cheats from the Extras menu. Enter ANTONIO.

ALL SINGLE-PLAYER MODERN MODE LEVELS
Select Cheats from the Extras menu. Enter Prohias.

MULTIPLAYER LEVELS
Select Cheats from the Extras menu. Enter MADMAG.

INVULNERABILITY
Select Cheats from the Extras menu. Enter ARMOR.

ALL SPY ATTACHMENTS
Select Cheats from the Extras menu. Enter DISGUISE.

PERMANENT FAIRY
Select Cheats from the Extras menu. Enter FAIRY.

SSX 3

CHEAT CHARACTERS

Select Options from the Main Menu. Choose Enter Cheat from the Options menu and enter the following codes to unlock each character. In the game, go to the Lodge and select Rider Details. Then select Cheat Characters to find the Cheat Characters.

CHARACTER	CODE
Brodi	zenmaster
Bunny San	wheresyourtail
Canhuck	greatwhitenorth
Churchill	tankengine
Cudmore	milkemdaisy
Eddie	worm
Gutless	boneyardreject
Hiro	slicksuit
Jurgen	brokenleg
Luther	bronco
Marty	back2future
NW Legend	callhimgeorge
Snowballs	betyouveneverseen
Stretch	windmilldunk
Svelte Luther	notsosvelte
Unknown Rider	finallymadeitin

OPEN ALL PEAKS
Enter biggerthank7.

PEAK 1 CLOTHES
Enter shoppingspree.

ALL PLAYLIST SONGS
Enter djsuperstar.

ALL POSTERS
Enter postnobills.

ALL ARTWORK
Enter naturalconcept.

ALL BOARDS
Enter graphicdelight.

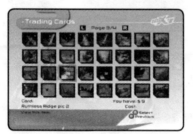

ALL TOYS
Enter nogluerequired.

ALL TRADING CARDS
Enter gotitgotitneedit.

ALL VIDEOS
Enter myeyesaredim.

STARSKY AND HUTCH

UNLOCK EVERYTHING
Enter VADKRAM as a profile name.

STAR WARS: BATTLEFRONT

SMALL PEOPLE
Create a profile named Jub Jub.

STAR WARS KNIGHTS OF THE OLD REPUBLIC II: THE SITH LORDS

CHANGE VOICES

Add a controller to the fourth port and press Black or White to raise and lower their voice.

STAR WARS REPUBLIC COMMANDO

GOD MODE
Pause the game and press Y, Y, Left Trigger, Up, X, Black, X, Y.

AMMO
Pause the game and press Y, Y, X, Down, Right trigger, Left trigger, Right trigger, Up.

TAZ WANTED

ALL LEVELS
At the start game screen, select Marvin the Martian and enter #OP.

ALL BONUS GAMES
At the start game screen, select Daffy Duck and enter ?BN.

2-PLAYER BOSS GAMES
At the start game screen, select Big red and enter *JC.

ART GALLERY
At the start game screen, select Tweety and enter .RT.

DISABLE WHACK IN THE BOXES
At the start game screen, select Taz and enter !WB.

TEENAGE MUTANT NINJA TURTLES 2: BATTLE NEXUS

Select Password from the Options menu and enter the following. Hold L while selecting a turtle to get his New Nexus Turtle outfit.

EFFECT	PASSWORD
Challenge Code Abyss	SDSDRLD
Challenge Code Endurance	MRMDRMD
Challenge Code Fatal Blow	LRSRDRD
Challenge Code Lose Shuriken	RLMRDSL
Challenge Code Nightmare	SLSDRDL
Challenge Code Poison	DRSLLSR
Challenge Code Super-Tough	RDSRMRL
Cheat Code All-You-Can-Throw Shuriken	RSRLRSM
Cheat Code Health	DSRDMRM
Cheat Code Mighty Turtle	LSDRRDR
Cheat Code Pizza Paradise	MRLMRMR
Cheat Code Self Recovery	DRMSRLR
Cheat Code Squeaking	MLDSRDM
Cheat Code Super Defense Power	LDRMRLM
Cheat Code Super Offense Power	SDLSRLL
Cheat Code Toddling	SSSMRDD
New Nexus Turtle outfit for Donatello	DSLRDRM
New Nexus Turtle outfit for Leonardo	LMRMDRD
New Nexus Turtle outfit for Michelangelo	MLMRDRM
New Nexus Turtle outfit for Raphael	RMSRMDR
Playmates added to Bonus Materials	SRMLDDR

TOM & JERRY: WAR OF THE WHISKERS

REFILL HEALTH
Select Game Cheats from the options and enter A, B, A, Y, Y, X, B, Y.

ALL COSTUMES AND CHARACTERS
Select Game Cheats from the options and enter B, B, A, X, B, Y, A, B.

ALL MAPS IN VERSUS
Select Game Cheats from the options and enter Y, B, Y, Y, A, X, B, X.

TIGER WOODS PGA TOUR 2005

Select Passwords from the Options menu and enter the following:

ALL GOLFERS AND COURSES
Enter THEGIANTOYSTER.

ALL COURSES
Enter THEWORLDISYOURS.

ALL ACCESSORIES
Enter TIGERMOBILE.

THE ROOF IN THE SKILLZONE GAME MODE
Enter NIGHTGOLFER.

JUSTIN TIMBERLAKE
Enter THETENNESSEEKID.

ARNOLD PALMER
Enter THEKING.

BEN HOGAN
Enter PUREGOLF

SEVE BALLESTEROS
Enter THEMAGICIAN

JACK NICKLAUS
Enter GOLDENBEAR.

GARY PLAYER
Enter BLACKKNIGHT.

TIFFANY "TIFF" WILLIAMSON
Enter RICHGIRL

JEB "SHOOTER" MCGRAW
Enter SIXSHOOTER

HUNTER "STEELHEAD" ELMORE
Enter GREENCOLLAR

ALASTAIR" CAPTAIN" MCFADDEN
Enter NICESOCKS

BEV "BOOMER" BUOUCHIER
Enter THEBEEHIVE

ADRIANA "SUGAR" DULCE
Enter SOSWEET

APHRODITE PAPADAPOLUS
Enter TEMPTING

BILLY "BEAR" HIGHTOWER
Enter TOOTALL

KENDRA "SPIKE" LOVETTE
Enter ENGLISHPUNK

DION "DOUBLE D" DOUGLAS
Enter DDDOUGLAS

RAQUEL "ROCKY" ROGERS
Enter DOUBLER

BUNJIRO "BUD" TANAKA
Enter INTHEFAMILY

CEASAR "THE EMPEROR" ROSADO
Enter LANDownER

REGINALD "REG" WEATHERS
Enter REGGIE

THE HUSTLER
Enter ALTEREGO

SUNDAY TIGER WOODS
Enter NEWLEGEND

ADIDAS ITEMS
Enter 91treSTR

CALLAWAY ITEMS
Enter cgTR78qw

CLEVELAND ITEMS
Enter CL45etUB

MAXFLI ITEMS
Enter FDGH597i

NIKE ITEMS
Enter YJHk342B

ODYSSEY ITEMS
Enter kjnMR3qv

PING ITEMS
Enter R453DrTe

PRECEPT ITEMS
Enter BRi3498Z

TAG ITEMS
Enter cDsa2fgY

TOURSTAGE ITEMS
Enter TS345329

TONY HAWK'S UNDERGROUND

Select Cheat Codes from the Options menu and enter the following codes. Pause the game and select Cheats from the Options menu to toggle the cheats on and off.

PERFECT RAIL
Enter **letitslide**.

PERFECT SKITCH
Enter **rearrider**.

PERFECT MANUAL
Enter **keepitsteady**.

MOON GRAVITY
Enter **getitup**.

TONY HAWK'S UNDERGROUND 2

Select Cheat Codes from the Game Options and enter the following. For the cheats, pause the game and select Cheats to turn them on.

NATAS KAUPAS
Enter bedizzy.

NIGEL BEAVERHOPUSEN
Enter skullet.

PAULIE RYAN
Enter 4wheeler.

PHIL MARGERA
Enter notvito.

ALL LEVELS
Enter accesspass.

ALWAYS SPECIAL CHEAT
Enter likepaulie.

PERFECT RAIL CHEAT
Enter straightedge.

ALL MOVIES
Enter frontrowseat.

TY THE TASMANIAN TIGER 2: BUSH RESCUE

ALL BUNYIP KEYS
During a game, press Start, Y, Start, Start, Y, X, B, X, A.

ALL FIRST-LEVEL RANGS
During a game, press Start, Y, Start, Start, Y, B, X, B, X.

ALL SECOND-LEVEL RANGS
During a game, press Start, Y, Start, Start, Y, X, B, X, Y.

GET 100,000 OPALS
During a game, press Start, Y, Start, Start, Y, B, A, B, A.

HIGHLIGHT ALL COLLECTIBLES CHEAT GNOME
During a game, press Left + Y + Down + A + X. Now you can enter the following cheats.

MAX ARTISTIC
Press Y, Down, BLACK, A, B.

MAX MENTAL
Press L, B, A, BLACK, Down.

MAX PHYSTICAL
Press L, R, A, Down, BLACK.

ACQUIRE SKILL
Press L, BLACK, Right, X, Left.

POWER SOCIAL
Press Down, BLACK, Right, X, Left.

TEAM PHOTO
At the credits screen, press Up, Down, X, Up, Down.

WORLD RACING

ALL CARS
Enter Full House as a name.

ALL TRACKS
Enter Free Ride as a name.

ALL MISSIONS
Enter Miss World as a name.

ALL CHAMPIONSHIPS
Enter JamSession as a name.

ALMOST EVERY CAR
Enter ALLUCANGET as a name.

STATUS 1
Enter Top 10 as a name.

STATUS 2
Enter HUIBUH as a name.

STATUS 3
Enter N.I.C.E. 2 as a name.

STATUS 4
Enter TaxiDriver as a name.

STATUS 5
Enter Halbzeit as a name.

STATUS 6
Enter No Hat! as a name.

STATUS 7
Enter McRace as a name.

STATUS 8
Enter Jiu-Jitsu as a name.

STATUS 9
Enter Goodzpeed as a name.

WRATH UNLEASHED

LARGE CHARACTERS
At the title screen, press Left, X, Up, Y, Right, B, Down, B.

DOUBLE HEALTH AND SPEED IN VERSUS AND TEAM FIGHER MODES
At the title screen, press Down, Down, Up, Down, Left, Right, Down, Up (x3), Right, Left, X.

ALTERNATE CHARACTERS IN VERSUS MODE
At the character select, press L, L, Down, Down, Black, White, Black, White, R, L, Black, R, R, White.

ALTERNATE CHARACTERS IN TEAM FIGHTER MODE
At the title screen, press L, L, Down, Down, Black, White, Black, White, R, L, Black, R (x3), White. Press the Black Button to for alternate characters.

XGRA: EXTREME-G RACING ASSOCIATION

ALL LEVELS OF RACING
Enter FREEPLAY at the Cheat Menu.

ALL TRACKS
Enter WIBBLE at the Cheat Menu.

O2 LIVERIED
Enter UCANDO at the Cheat Menu.

MESSAGE IN CREDITS
Enter MUNCHKIN, EDDROOLZ or EDDIEPOO at the Cheat Menu.

YAGER

ALL LEVELS
Enter lvl.activate 1 as a profile name.

9 CONTINUES
Enter set MAXCNT 9 as a profile name.

COMPLETE DATABASE
Enter data.setvis 1 as a profile name.

YU-GI-OH! THE DAWN OF DESTINY

COSMO QUEEN CARD IN DECK
Enter your name as KONAMI.

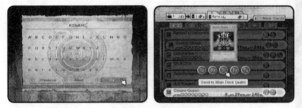

TRI-HORN DRAGON CARD IN DECK
Enter your name as HEARTOFCARDS.

ZERA THE MANT CARD IN DECK
Enter your name as XBOX.

ZAPPER

UNLIMITED LIVES
Pause the game, hold L and press Up, Up, Up, Left, Left, Right, Left, Right.

UNLIMITED SHIELD
Pause the game, hold L and press Up, Down, Up, Left, Right, Down, Up.

SECRET CODES 2005 VOL. 2

©2005 Pearson Education

BradyGAMES® is a registered trademark of Pearson Education, Inc.

All rights reserved, including the right of reproduction in whole or in part in any form.

BradyGAMES® Publishing

An Imprint of Pearson Education
800 East 96th Street, Third Floor
Indianapolis, Indiana 46240

ISBN: 0-7440-0550-7

Printing Code: The rightmost double-digit number is the year of the book's printing; the rightmost single-digit number is the number of the book's printing. For example, 05-1 shows that the first printing of the book occurred in 2005.

08 07 06 05   4 3 2 1

Manufactured in the United States of America.

BRADYGAMES STAFF

Publisher
David Waybright

Licensing Manager
Mike Degler

Director of Marketing
Steve Escalante

Editor-In-Chief
H. Leigh Davis

Creative Director
Robin Lasek

Assistant Marketing Manager
Susie Nieman

Assistant Marketing Manager, Online
Rachel Wolfe

Marketing Coordinator
Autumne Bruce

Team Coordinator
Stacey Beheler

BOOK CREDITS

Senior Development Editor
Ken Schmidt

Screenshot Editor
Michael Owen

Book Designer
Dan Caparo

Production Designer
Wil Cruz